Jokester

By

Hugh Jass
and
Mike Krotch

NSFW, children or church ladies.

ISBN-13: 978-1477536957

A COLLECTION OF JOKES FOR THE POLITICALLY INCORRECT! CAUTION! IF YOU ARE OFFENDED BY POOR TASTE, BIGOTS, SEXISM AND RACISM; DO NOT READ THE FOLLOWING PAGES. CAUTION!

On the chest of a barmaid named Gail,
Was tattooed the prices of ale
And on her behind
For the sake of the blind,
Was the very same thing in Braille!

According to the National Enquirer great sex melts the wax in your ears.

Examination of rudimentary mathematics indicates LSD x IBM = a business trip.

A guy was at a costume party dressed as a mushroom. Another was dressed as a piece of shit with a Star Trek logo on it. "I see that you are dressed as a mushroom."
"No, I'm a Fun-guy. What are you?"
"The Captain's Log."

Nymphomaniacal Jill,
Tried a dynamite stick for a thrill.
They found her vagina
In North Carolina
And bits of her tits in Brazil!

A naive newlywed bride goes to the doctor to find out about her husband's anatomy. "What's the dangly bit between his legs?"
"That is called the penis."
"And the bump on the end?"
"The head of the penis." says the doctor.
"And the two round things 12 inches back from the head of the penis?"

"Well I don't know about your husband Ma'am," said the doctor "but on me those are the cheeks of my ass!"

What has three wheels and goes around underwater? A motorpike with a side carp.

A woman is watching her man undress for the first time. He takes his socks off revealing malformed feet. "What happened to your feet?" she asks

"I had toelio when I was a kid." He gives her a kiss and then drops his trousers. She looks at his legs "What happened to your knees?"

"Kneesles." he said and drops his underwear. "Oh let me guess," she said "Small cox?"

How is an elephant and a Seiko watch the same? They both come in quarts.

This guy goes from the bush to a fine restaurant and is refused service because he is not wearing a tie. He looks in his car for one and only finds a set of battery jumper cables. Putting those on he goes back to the restaurant where the maitre d' looks at him and the jumper cables around his neck and says " O.K. I'll let you in; just don't start anything."

A mother takes her frail teenage daughter to the doctor. The daughter has been constantly ill and in and out of doctor's offices. After looking at the girl the doctor comes out and asks the mother "Has your daughter ever had intercourse?"

"No" sighs the mother "but she has had everything else. You might as well give her that too."

Did you hear about the guy going around putting dynamite in kitchens? His name was Linoleum Blownapart.

The guy who refused Novocain at the dentist decided to transcend dental medication.

The taxidermist whose arm kept moving up and down? He was the hare restorer with a permanent wave.

The name of the Hindu coat checker? M'hat M'coat.

If it were raining naked women, with my luck I'd get a lesbian.

How long is the "hair" on the rabbit? About 2 seconds.

What was white and had a black asshole? The A Team.

I was so poor that I couldn't even pay attention.

What do you get if your donkey swallows the legs of my rooster?
Two feet of my cock up your ass.

Test tube babies have designer genes and a womb with a view.

What goes click, click, click. Is that it? Click, click, click. Is that it? Click, click, click. Is that it? Click, click, click. Is that it? Stevie Wonder doing Rubik's Cube.

What is the fastest bird alive? The Ethiopian chicken.

What do you call an Ethiopian with a dog? A vegetarian.

A Pole and a Czech go hiking and are eaten by bears. The bears are found and the female is shot but the male gets away. They cut open the female and find the remains of the Pole. One cop says, "I guess that means that the Czech is in the male."
What is the German word for virgin? Fitzgudantite.

G.A.Y. = Got Aids Yet

M.A.G.I.C. Johnson = My Ass Got Infected Coach

What kinds of animals live in a pair of stockings? Ten little piggies, two calves, one ass, one beaver, many "hares" and a fish that nobody can find.

Want to speak Newfie? Whale oil beef hooked. Corksucking, farging icehole.

What is a twenty-minute workout for a Chinese? Parallel parking.

What did the elephant say when he was pulled out of the ditch by the Balls?
"Thank you, Mr. and Mrs. Ball."

NEWS ITEM - Space Shuttle Challenger explodes killing all seven astronauts including a schoolteacher.

What did she teach? History.

What was the last thing that she said? "Hey what's this button do?"

What does NASA mean? Need Another Seven Astronauts.

When is the next launch? July 4.

Where do the astronauts go for vacations? All over Florida.

What is the difference between mono and aids? You get mono by snatching kisses.

Did you hear about the Ku Klux Klan chain saw? Start it up and it goes "Run nigger, nigger, nigger."

Why are there no Polish floatplane pilots? They all drowned on the walk around inspection.

What do ten thousand battered women have in common? They didn't know when to shut the fuck up.

They just built a new shelter. Its called Tempura House. It's for lightly battered women.

What do you call a tree full of naked women? A country.

Newfie takes his first flight over the ocean. The engines fail and the captain tells everyone to assume the crash position. The Negro stewardess walks down the aisle making sure that everyone is doing the right thing when the Newfie grabs her and starts having sex. One of the passengers asks him if he should be doing that. "Ah tell ye boy" says the Newfie "if we are going to crash like the captain says then I want to be in the safest place possible and I hear that the black box always survives the crash."

Did you hear about Evil Knievel's latest? He is going to try and make it across Newfoundland dressed as a choirboy.

WHAT DO YOU CALL A GUY WITH NO ARMS AND NO LEGS...
in a gravel pit? Phil.
in a pressure cooker? Stu.
outside your door? Matt.
on water skis? Skip.
inside a bun? Frank.
hanging by your window? Kurt and Rod.
on your wall? Art.
in the middle of the lake? Bob.
in a pile of leaves? Russell.

a matador with no arms or legs? Gord.

What do the Waltons call their gardener? Lawn-boy.

... their dog? Here-boy.

... their athletic son? Gym-bag.

What do you call a dog with no legs? It doesn't matter; he won't come anyway.

... a cow with no legs? Ground beef.

... a cow with two left legs? Lean ground beef.

... a girl with half her leg missing? Ilene.

... a chinese girl with half her leg missing? Irene.

... a girl with one leg? Peg

What do you get when you cross a penis with a potato? A dictator.

There is nothing more curious than a woman who isn't.

Did you hear about the two Irish homosexuals? Patrick Fitzgerald and Gerald Fitzpatrick.

The two Scottish homosexuals? Ben Doon and Philip McRevice.

Why were women invented? Because sheep don't do dishes.

Why do women have one more brain cell then a cow? So they don't shit on the floor when they do the dishes.

Excuses are like assholes. Everyone has one and they all stink.

Did you hear the one about the honest politician? Neither did I.

How did break dancing start? Newfie kids stealing hubcaps from moving cars.

Why don't men like crotch less panties? Because their balls hang out.

What were the last three movies Rock Hudson made before he died of AIDS? Rambutt, Romancing the Bone and Germs of Endearment.

Virgins use vaseline; whores use polygrip.

A guy goes parachuting and both his chutes fail. To his amazement as he falls towards earth he sees a guy coming up at him. "Hey do you know how to work a parachute?" he asks. "No. Do you know how to work a Coleman stove?"

Why do they wrap their hamsters in duct tape on Davie Street? So it doesn't explode when they fuck it.

Who has killed more Indians than General Custer? Union Carbide. (Bhophal, India)

Muskox come from musk eggs.

English Tea. Darjeeling tea-10% substance, 90% aroma.
Earl Grey tea-90% substance, 10% aroma.
Orange Pekoe tea- definitely preferred.
Texas T   F-A-R-T 10% substance, 90% aroma.
S-H-I-T 90% substance, 10% aroma.
C-U-N-T definitely preferred.

A man might look forty but it is hard to tell his IQ at a glance.

Where does all the white go when the snow melts?

Two farmers watch an aircraft fly over with a cargo door open and stuff falling out. Little engine parts from Datsun. "You know Ernie," says one as he picked up a piece and saw datsun written on it "I've been here a long time but this is the first time that I've seen it rain Datsun cogs."

A chieftain was given a great big throne but had no room in his hut for it so he put it up in the rafters. The grass hut wasn't strong enough to support it and the throne crashed down and killed him. The moral: Never stow thrones in grass houses.

This nun is really hot working all alone in the nunnery. So she takes off her clothes and feels much cooler. The gate keeper phones and says that there is a blind man coming up to see her. She doesn't worry about putting on her clothes because it's a blind man. There is a knock on the door and the blind man walks in and says "Nice tits lady. Where do you want these blinds hung?"

If a native indian couple get divorced does that mean they can still be cousins?

Fat man on the bus says to the little boy "Why don't you be a gentleman and give up your seat for a lady?" The little boy says "Why don't you be a gentleman and give up your seat for two ladies?"

Biker says to the waitress "I'd like to fuck you on this bar." She says, "Don't talk like that or I'll get my boyfriend." Biker says, "I'd like to flip you upside down, fill your pussy full of beer and drink it all out." She goes to get her boyfriend and tells him "That biker said he wanted to fuck me on the bar." The boyfriend rolls up his sleeves. Then she says, "He wants to fill my pussy full of beer and drink it all out." He rolls down his sleeves. She says, "Aren't you going to punch him out?" "No way" says the boyfriend "I'm not going to mess with anyone who can drink that much beer!"

Two gays are at the zoo and see a gorilla beating off. One of them backs up to the cage with his pants down hoping to get some. The gorilla grabs him and drags him into the cage and does him big time. The next day one asks the other "Are you hurt?" "You bet. He hasn't called or written since we did it."

What has 100 balls and fucks rabbits? A shotgun.

What is long and hard on a black man? Grade 2.

NEWS ITEM: A dismembered man found stuffed into an East Indian owned pizzeria.

They found out who it was; Amere Cinder. Although it could have been Pan Deep. The new pizza is hands and pineapple but it is expensive; it costs an arm and a leg.

Real estate salesmen a.k.a. house pimps.

The new T-shirt; On the front is "Earth First" on the back it says "We'll log the other planets later."

Another has a picture of a red and white Campbell's soup can listing the contents as Cream of Spotted Owl.

What do you call a hooker with a runny nose? Full.

The tax collector is talking to the hooker. "I made $100,000 last year and had 50 collectors working for me." he says." Well," replies the hooker "I made $200,000 last year and only had one cunt working for me."

One farmer says to the other "When we first got married it was like a birds nest. Now after six kids it looks like a cow pie with a wagon track through it."

That town was so redneck they are thinking of having the Homophobic Olympics.

Quasimoto was getting old so he put an ad in the paper for a replacement. A midget with no arms shows up. "How can you work the bells?" "Easy" says the midget as he takes a run at the bell and hits it with his head. BONG! He backs up and does it again. BONG! The third time he misses and runs off the edge. SPLAT! Onto the cobbles below. Quasimoto humps down the stairs to where a crowd has gathered around the midget. A bystander asks "Do you know this guy?" "No" says Quasimoto "but his face sure rings a bell."

That pilot - is he a fog ducking smart feller, or the other way around, a dog fucking fart smeller?

What do you call the cheese grater guy? The hinder binder grinder minder.

What has 18 eyes and catches flies? A baseball team.

Canadian Women in Timber is not to be outdone by their gay counterparts : Canadian Lesbians in Timber also known as C.L.I.T.

What weighs 600 pounds is yellow and flies? Two 300-pound canaries.

Did you hear the one about the three Canadians and the white guy?

Did you hear that the Newfies bought some septic tanks and as soon as they figure out how to drive them, they will attack Quebec.

How about the cowboy who sowed his wild oats on Saturday night and then on Sunday morning prayed for a crop failure.

How well does a woman hold her liquor? Tightly by the ears.

A protester fell out of a big cedar tree and got a branch stuck up her bum. The doctor was not allowed to remove it as it was an old growth tree too close to a recreation area.

The secretary asks the boss "May I use your dictaphone?"
"No, use your finger like everyone else."

Male chauvinist pig definition of love "The white stuff that comes out the end of my dick."

Golfer wants to know if there is golfing in heaven so he goes to a fortuneteller. She says come back tomorrow. He does. She says, "I have good news and bad news. The good news is that, yes they do have a golf course in heaven. The bad news is that you have a tee off time of two o'clock today.

If there are two people in an elevator and one of them farts; both know who did it.

If there are two people and a dog in an elevator and one of the people farts; they both look at the dog.

How is Michael Jackson and whiskey the same? They both come in tots.

Did you hear about the trapeze artist who divorced his wife? He caught her in the act.

What did Jeffrey Dahmer say to Louise Bobbitt? "Are you going to eat that?"

Joe comes to work with a hoarse voice. "Got it golfing. " he says.
"Hooked the ball off the fifteenth into a cow pasture. Looked all over for it. Then I saw a cow standing kind of strange so I walked over and lifted the tail. Sure enough there was a golf ball; but it was a Titleist - not my ball. Then I see this lady walking around in the same pasture so I lift up the cow's tail and say - Hey lady, does this look like yours? I got a nine iron right across the throat."

A guy says to the Newfie cook "I've got a bunch of friends coming over and we need a lot of food. Take this recipe and double it." The Newfie looks at the recipe and says, " I can't."

"Why not?" says the guy "All you have to do is double the recipe."
"I'd like to help you me son" says the Newfie "but my oven doesn't go up to 700 degrees."

Two women were out in the garden pulling carrots. "Oh this one looks like my husband," says one. "Why?" says the other "Because it is so long and hard?"
"No. Its because its dirty and covered with hairs."

Goober comes home to find Martha packing. "Where are you going?" "I'm going to Las Vegas where they pay $400 for what I give you for nothing!" Goober starts packing. "What are you doing?" asks Martha.
"I'm going to Vegas to watch you live on $800 a year!"

Yellow snow a.k.a. Indian slurpee.

Why are they called apartments if they are so close together?

Tell me son do you know what a penis is? Sure. It's the guy who plays the piano.

What do they do with used tampons in Surrey? Bingo blotters.

This guy comes in from the bush and has great sex with his wife. The next morning she says " We haven't done a 69 for a long time. Lets do it." They go at it for a while then the doorbell rings. He jumps up, puts on his housecoat and answers the door. His best friend is there and says "Sorry, didn't mean to interrupt your breakfast." "How can you tell? Jam on my mouth?" " No. Peanut butter on your forehead."

What do they pack Styrofoam in when they ship it?

How are floor tiles and men the same? Lay them right the first time and you can walk on them forever.

On their 25th wedding anniversary a husband and wife were naked in the same hotel room as on their honeymoon. The husband looks at his wife and says, "Have you ever thought about all the things we accomplished?" "Like what?" she says. "When I first saw you naked" he says, "all I wanted to do was suck your tits dry and screw your brains out and now look at you 25 years later!"

Did you hear about the two four year old boys who tried to buy a box of tampons because they heard their older sister saying you could swim, ride bicycles and horses once you had them.

The holy of holies - colletus uninteruptus; slipping her the old salami; putting the hot dog in the bun; a tomcat on the prowl; taking the log to the beaver; burying the boner; taking the skinboat to Tunatown; taking a ride on the wild baloney pony.

O.J. Simpson is to remarry. He wants to take another stab at it.

Knock knock. Who's there? O.J. O.J. who? Congratulations you are on the jury.

The convicts in the prison won't let O.J. play baseball because he can't find his bloody glove.

O.J. comes to court wearing sandals, shorts, Hawaiian shirt and a sombrero. The lawyer says "You misunderstood me. I said you are going to the can, coon.

"Grandpa makes a sound like a frog." "Why should I my boy?" " Because Grandma says when you croak we're all going to Hawaii!"

Honey let's make love. No, I'm going to the gynecologist tomorrow and I will be embarrassed if he sees we have been doing it. Honey let's make out. No I told you why. Its o.k. you're not going to the dentist!

They have a new camera out called the Hemorrhoid. Now even assholes can take lots and lots of shitty pictures.

Hear about that guy with wooden legs? He caught fire and burnt to the ground.
The Newfie comes from the phone crying. "My father just died." An hour later he comes back from another phone call crying. "Its a terrible day. My brother's father just died too."

If water is made of hydrogen and oxygen why doesn't it burn? Because it is too wet.

Two termites walk into a pub and ask " Is the bar tender here?"

Two guys walk into a bar. One ducks.

What's the difference between a hooker with diarrhea and an oyster shucker with epilepsy? One shucks between fits.

How are women and dogshit the same? The older they are the easier they are to pick up.

Why do they bury lawyers at sea? Because deep down they're all good guys.

A guy goes to court and the Judge asks, "Where is your lawyer?" The man replies, "I don't need one your Honour. I'm going to tell the truth."

This golfer dies and goes to heaven. At the gates Saint Peter leans out the window and says "Anything to declare?"

The golfer says "I feel sorry because I took the Lord's name in vain.".

"Hmm." said St.Peter "Taking the Lord's name in vain is bad. Tell me about it.".

"I was on the eighteenth tee playing the best game of my life. I teed off and drove the ball straight into a sand trap."

"And then you took the Lord's name in vain?" said St.Peter

"No. I got out the sand wedge and chipped it up onto the green stopping four inches from the cup."

"And then you took the Lord's name in vain?" said St. Peter

"No, not then." says the golfer

"Jesus Christ, you didn't miss a four inch putt?"

What do the good ol' boys in Texas call Negro skydivers? Skeet.

What is the difference between Christopher Reeves and O.J. Simpson? O.J. will walk.

Did you hear that Disney is making a movie about the Simpson trial? It will be called the Lying Coon.

The NFL is to paint the football green and silver. Have you ever seen a black guy drop a watermelon or a hubcap?

FORD = Found On Road Dead

PONTIAC = Poor Old Newfie Thinks Its A Cadillac

Chinese word for heifer = Youngcow

Why do women wear makeup and perfume? Because they are ugly and they smell bad.

What has 7 teeth and is twelve feet long? A native road blockade.

Do you realize that when you smell a fart that something from inside someone's asshole and is now inside your head?

Chretien comes to Terrace and wears a windbreaker "Because my aid said wear a windbreaker." He goes to Kitimat wearing a raincoat "Because my aide said wear a raincoat." He goes to Kemano wearing a fox hat "Because my aid said where the fuck's that?"

What did the prostitute sing to the cowboy? "Get it up. Get it in. Get it out. Don't mess my hairdo."

How many reasons are there for a woman to be in the cockpit of an aircraft? Three, if she takes it up the ass.

Forty years they've been married and she never looked in the tea chest. When she did there were six empty Coke bottles and $4,000. Why? Every time he was unfaithful he drank a Coke and put the bottle in the chest. He kept the money from the returned empties too.

What did the banana say to the vibrator? What are you shaking for she is going to eat me.

Paleontologists have found two new dinosaurs - both homosexual. The lesbian they have named Lickalottapus and the gay male they named Megasoreass.

What do you call a dinosaur with a large vocabulary? A Thesaurus.

What is the difference between a Rolling Stones song and a Scotsman? The song is "Hey, you! Get off of my cloud!" and the Scotsman says "Hey McLeod! Get off of my ewe!"

Why do doctors slap newborn babies? To knock the balls off the stupid ones.

Stand six shovels up against a wall and confuse a Newfie. Tell him to take his pick.

Why do witches ride their brooms with no panties on? To get a better grip.

Tact: The ability to describe people as they see themselves.

The new $2 is truly Canadian; it is always threatening to separate.

They will call the coin Moonie because it is a picture of the Queen with a bear behind.

Why do lawyers float? Because they are scum.

Strange goings on in a manor house in England. The lady of the house goes into the servant's room unannounced. She says to the servant "Come here and take off my dress." and he does. "Now take off my shoes." and he does." Now take off my corset... and take off my brassiere...and take off my panties." He does all this and then she says "And don't ever let me catch you wearing my clothes again."

A man should never argue with his wife - if anything he should dicker.

An airline pilot dies and goes to hell. Behind the devil there are three doors. When the devil turns his back to answer a phone the pilot looks in them. The first door is pilots doing eternal walk around daily inspections. The second door has pilots dealing with emergencies but behind the third door is pilots being served and attended to constantly by flight attendants. He tells the devil he wants the third door. "You can't have it" says the devil "that is flight attendant hell."

What is the difference between a clitoris and a golf ball? A man will spend up to ten minutes looking for a golf ball.

Parbit Scinder is working at the East Indian flour factory when a bin opens and covers him in flour. He has to go home and shower. His co-workers, his boss, the secretary, the gardener all ask him what happened. When he gets home and his wife asks him what happened he explodes in rage and frustration saying " I've only been white for an hour and already you Hindus are starting to piss me off."

How do you know when a blonde is going to say something intelligent? She starts by saying " My husband told me..."

How do you make three pounds of fat edible? Put a nipple on it.

A guy walks up to the counter and says give me two pounds of Polish Sausage. The clerk asks him if he is Polish. "Why do you ask me that?" says the Pole "Why not German or Ukrainian or Japanese?" The clerk replies, "Because this is a hardware store."

What is the difference between a wife and a washing machine? You don't have to hug your washing machine for half an hour after you put your load in.

TWA crashes into the ocean. What does one Coast Guard guy say to another? "You should have seen the piece of ass I picked up last night."

The miracle of AIDS turns fruits into vegetables.

How is a tornado and a woman the same? They both scream when they are coming and they both take your car and your house when they leave.

Why do black men have long penises? It is God's way of apologizing for putting pubic hair on their head.

What do the good ol boys in Alabama do for fun on Hallowe'en? Pumpkin.

What does a Mennonite wear to rob someone? Robber boots.

Why do East Indians in the lower mainland have big noses? So they have something to pick in the winter.

How do you know that the toothbrush was invented by a native? If it was a white guy it would have been a teethbrush.

A man wins millions of dollars. "What do you want?" he says to his oldest son." A trip around the world." "What do you want?" he says to his teenaged son." A car." So he buys him a Maserati. "What do you want?" he says to his preschooler." A Mickey Mouse Outfit". So he buys him your company.

Did you hear about the new lesbian house? Its all tongue in groove without a stud in the place.

Lesbians new operation is strapadicktomy. Nymphomaniacs get a Sticadicktomy.

Why is a blond like a turtle? Once they are on their back they are screwed.

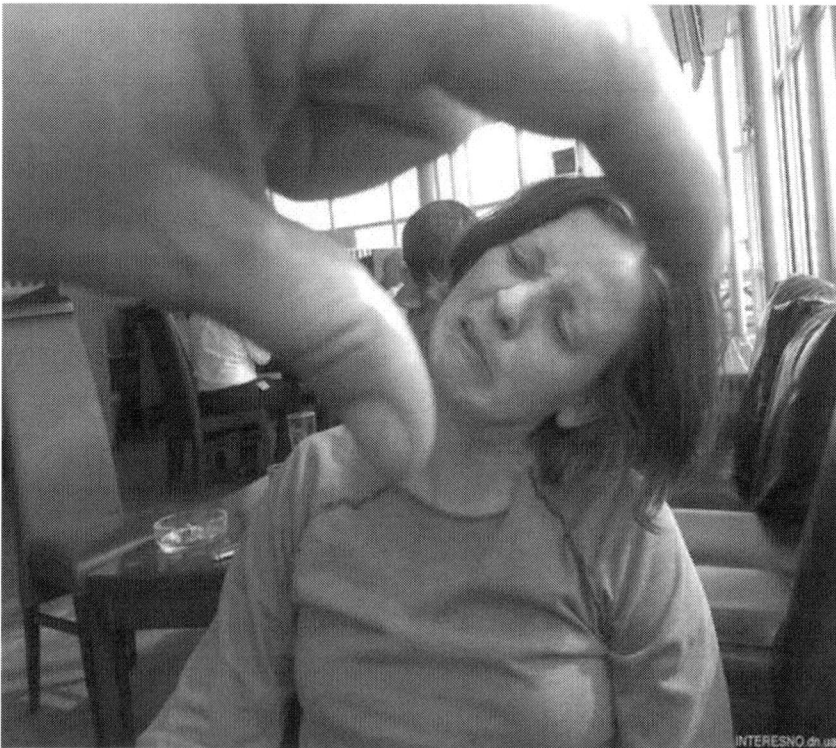

What do you get if you take the ears off a bear? B.

What does a blonde say when she gives birth? Are you sure its mine?

How do you kill a blonde? Put spikes on her shoulder pads.

Captains are capable of warm and caring feelings. They just don't involve anyone else.

Flying along in a 747 the captain dies. The Purser asks the first officer "What are we going to do?" The co-pilot replies "The first thing we do is get him out of MY seat!"

Did you hear about four year old Jim? He was bugging his mother so she said "Jimmy, why don't you go across the street and watch the builders work. Maybe you will learn something." Jimmy was gone about two hours. When he came home his mother asked him what he had learned. Jimmy replied, " Well first you put the God Damn door up. Then the Son of a Bitch doesn't fit, so you take the cocksucker back down. Then you have to take a cunt hair off of each side and put the motherfucker back up." Jimmy's mother said, "You just wait until your father comes home." When Jimmy's Dad got home, Mom told him to ask Jimmy what he had learned across the street. Jimmy told him the whole story. Dad said, "Jimmy you go outside and get me a switch." Jimmy replied, "Fuck you, that's the electrician's job."

What is a Jewish conundrum? Free ham.

Why do men ejaculate so many sperm? Because none of them will ask directions.

The married couple named Dicky had a big fight. She cut his ears and hands off with a knife. The policewoman Loreena Bobbitt came to investigate and said "Why did you Missus Dicky?"

What is the difference between a circus and a line of chorus girls? The circus is a cunning array of stunts.

Why should you not eat out your girl friend after a night of sex? Ever tried to open up a day old grilled cheese sandwich?

If there are women only in the front of the aircraft it is called a box office.

Dead dog taken to the vet who proves it by passing a cat over it. Charged for office visit $50 and $450 for cat scan.

First year of marriage - house sex. Fifth year - bedroom sex. Tenth year - hallway sex, pass each other and say, "Fuck you".

A famous Duchess gave a dinner party to the cream of society. At dinner she let out a ripper of a fart and quick as a flash she turned her gaze to her stoic butler, standing as always, behind her.
"Hawkins" She cried. "Stop that!"
"Certainly your Grace," he replied with unhurried dignity. "Which way did it go?"

What is the difference between pink and purple? Her grip.

On a multi city tour of America the Pope finally gets to drive the car. Stopped for speeding. Cop calls in and says, "I've stopped a big one. I don't know who it is but he has the Pope for a chauffeur."

At a contest for farting in Bute
One lady's exertion was cute.
It won the diploma
For foetid aroma,
And three judges were felled by the brute!

Woman is God's second blunder - Nietzsche

What do you call a Portuguese woman with no legs?
Consuelo.

What do you call the children of a prostitute? Brothel
sprouts.

What three two letter words mean small? Is it in?

What's the motto at Amsterdam's Lesbian Convention?
Plug the Dyke!

How do you tell when a blonde has had a date? The
impression on her forehead of a belt buckle.

Pick a number between 2 and 10. Multiply it by 9. Add the two digits of the product together. Subtract 5. Use the number to find the corresponding letter of the alphabet (1 = A, 2 = B, 3 = C, etc.). Pick a country that begins with that letter. Pick an animal that begins with the second letter of the country. It is either an elephant in Denmark or an orangutan in Dominican Republic.

Two condoms walk by a gay bar. One says to the other "Let's go in there and get shit faced."

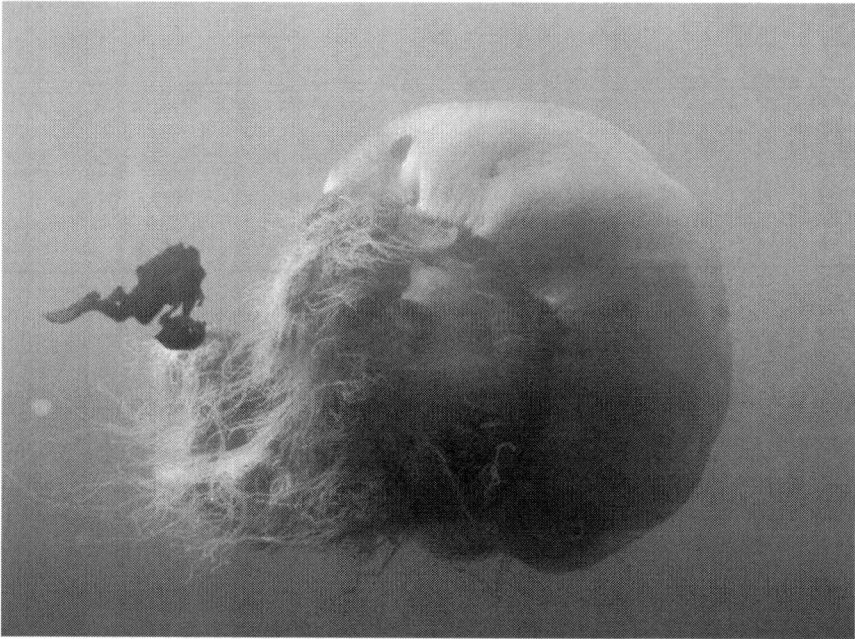

There is a house of ill repute (i.e. a cat house, whorehouse, red light district) on top of a hill. There are three guys - one running up the hill, one walking down the hill, and one inside the house. Where are these guys from? The guy running up the hill - him a Russian. The guy walking down the hill, him a Finnish. The guy in the house - Himalayan!

There was a 747 going across the Atlantic when it ran out of fuel half way there. The captain comes over the p.a. and says they are going to crash and die. One of the woman passengers loses it, stands up, rips her blouse off and says "Won't some man treat me like a real woman before I die?" A guy comes up to her, looks her meaningfully in the eye, rips his shirt off and says, "Iron this!"

Why don't cannibals eat clowns? Because they taste funny.

Rita MacNeill has a map of Canada tattooed across her bum. Every time she sits down Quebec separates.

Client: Listen I need legal advice but I don't have much money. What is your minimum charge?
Lawyer: One hundred dollars for three questions.
Client: Gosh, don't you think that's pretty steep?
Lawyer: Not really. What's your last question?

What is the difference between ignorance and complacency? I don't know and I don't care.

Did you hear about the new blonde paint? It's not real bright, it's cheap and it spreads easy.

What is a blonde's favourite nursery rhyme? Hump me, Dump me.

What is it when a man talks dirty to a woman? Sexual harassment. What is it when a woman talks dirty to a man? $3.99 a minute.

How do we know God is a man? Because if God was a woman, sperm would taste like chocolate.

A union shop steward goes to Nevada and wants to get laid. After looking a long time for a union bordello he finds one. " What is the percentage take here?" he asks. " House gets 20% the girl gets 80%." The madam says. "Great I'll take the young good looking blonde in the corner" "I'm sorry" says the madam "but you will have to take the fat ugly old one. She has seniority."

PARTIES
The more they drink, the less clothes they will wear.

Photoshopsquad.com

Tyrone the Negro kid comes home from grade two and says "Mom, how come my penis is so much bigger than all the other kids?" His mom snaps back "Because you are eighteen, Tyrone!"

Why does the bride wear white? So the dishwasher will match the rest of the appliances.

Just before the last referendum Lucien Bouchard decides he needs a King for the new country that will be Quebec. He picks a guy at random and phones him up. "I have to ask you some qualifying questions before I make you King. First, who is the greatest hockey team in the world?"

"The Montreal Canadiens"

"Good. Now who is the greatest hockey player ever?"

"Rocket Richard."

"Very good. Now because you will be representing a young and virile new country, you have to be virile too. How many times a week do you make love?"

"Three maybe four times."

"Oh no this is not good. It should be more like ten or twelve."

"Well I thought that 3-4 times was not bad for a priest in a small town with no car."

Three guys rob a bank and run away and hide in a barn. When the police come they each jump into a burlap bag. The police poke at the bags. The first one says, "Bow wow." The cops think it's a sack full of dogs. The second one says "Meow." The cops think it is a sack full of cats. The third one says "Po-Ta-To"

Why is aspirin white? Because they want it to work.

Why did the blonde go to Israel? Because she heard that Jesus was hung like this (hold out arms).

What do you call an intelligent blonde? A Golden Retriever.

What do you tell a blonde with two black eyes? Nothing, she has been told twice already.

Cowboy goes to heaven and St.Peter ells him he must answer three questions. How many days of the week start with the letter T. Two says the cowboy, Today and tomorrow. How many seconds are there in a year? 12. January second, February second...What is Gods first name? Andy. From the song And He walks with me...

Ever hear of Pizza Hut saying that your pizza is right or its free? How can a pizza be right? You would have to be a philosophy major to prove it. "Hey man, this pizza is burnt." you say to the waiter who replies "That's right."

A couple were celebrating the 20th wedding anniversary and the husband said "Let's drink to 20 years of faithfulness." The wife says "Let's not."
"What do you mean?" says the husband

"Well, to be truthful there were three times I wasn't faithful. Remember when we were just starting out and we needed a mortgage really bad? We were turned down and then the next day we got it."
"Oh well, that's OK. What about the second time?" he says.
"Remember when had to renew and we couldn't get a very good rate then the next day we got it?"
"Oh well, that's OK. What about the third time?" he says.
"Remember when you were running for president of the union local and you were 57 votes short of winning?"

It's hard being a dick. You have a head that can't think, an eye that can't see, you hang around with a couple of nuts, your closest neighbour is an asshole, your best friend is a pussy and your owner beats you all the time.

Two blondes look at some tracks in the snow. "That's rabbit tracks," says one. "No its coyote tracks" says the other. They argue like that until the train runs them over.

An American redneck is standing behind a couple of Japanese business men in California getting more and more frustrated as he listens to them talk in Japanese. Finally he explodes "GODAMN IT! This is America for Christ sakes - speak Spanish!"

On a flight from New York to L.A. a blonde sits in First Class with an Economy ticket. Flight attendant and purser try to get her to move but she won't until the captain whispers in her ear. What did he say? "This part of the plane doesn't go to L.A."

Question: How many feminists does it take to screw in a light bulb?
Answer: That's not funny.

How does Bill Gates of Microsoft screw in a light bulb? He doesn't. He declares dark to be the industry standard.

Straight guy walks into a gay bar and asks for a beer. "Sorry, but you have to name your penis before we serve you" says the gay bartender. "That's stupid but I want a beer. What did you name yours?" asks the guy.
"Nike - from the TV commercial you know- Just Do It" says the barkeep.
"OK I'll call mine Secret. Strong enough for a man but made for a woman."

How do you get a dog to stop humping your leg? Pick him up and suck him off.

What do you call a German proctologist? Hans Zinderhol.

Hear about the woman who got the inside of her thighs tattooed? Santa on the left and a turkey on the right. Now her husband can't complain that there is nothing to eat between Thanksgiving and Christmas.

What do you see when you look into a blonde's eyes? The back of her head.

Guy was in Prince Rupert for three days and it never stopped raining. He asks a kid if it ever stops raining and the kid says "How would I know - I'm only eight years old."

How many DC 3 pilots does it take to screw in a light bulb? Three - one to do it and two to talk about how good the old one was.

Woman goes to the doctor complaining that she farts all the time but they don't make noise or smell. He gives her pills. She's back next day complaining that her farts smell terrible. He says "Now that we have cleared your sinuses lets fix your hearing."

Big burly guy comes out of the bush and says "The first thing I am going to do when I get home is rip my wife's panties off. They are riding up the crack of my ass!"

Santa Claus was getting his annual check ride from Transport Canada. After doing all his paperwork, Santa does the pre-flight checking his reindeer and sled. As he is getting into the sled for the flight test he notices that the examiner is climbing in with a shotgun. "What's that for?" Santa asks incredulously. The examiner winked and said, "I'm not supposed to tell you this, but you're going to lose an engine on take off."

Why do gays wear ribbed condoms? Better traction in the mud.

A guy was driving through a reserve when his motor threw a rod. Some natives pull up beside him and ask what the problem is. "A piston broke." he says. "Yeah, us too. Pissed and broke."

Native has a kid. Nurse admires her and says, "What are you going to name her?"
"I'll call her Susie - like all her 5 other sisters."
"Isn't that confusing?"
"No its great if I want a beer I say Susie get me a beer. Or if I want the house cleaned I say Susie clean the house"
"What if you want to talk to just one specifically?"

"I call them by their last names."

Woman has a kid. As she is giving birth it comes out feet first. The doctor says "A very black footed kid"
"Yeah that's Jerome he is a great lover"
The doctor says, "What's this? The middle of the kid is white."
"Yeah that's Billy. He takes good care of me."
The doctor says, "What's this? The kid has the head of an oriental."
"Oh Thank goodness. I thought that you were going to say a head of a dog."

Did you hear about the gay guy who went on the patch? He is down to two butts a day.

Three guys with dogs. First is Engineer says to dog "T Square, DO!" Dog draws a circle. Very good says all. Chemist says to dog "Measure, DO!" Dog goes to fridge gets milk pours out exactly 8 ounces. Very good says all. Government worker says to dog "Coffee Break, DO!" Dog jumps up steals some cookies from the other guys, drinks the milk, dumps on the paper, screwed the other two dogs, claimed he injured his back, filed a grievance report for unsafe working conditions, put in for worker's comp and went home on sick leave.

Monica Lewinsky is getting a government pension for all the time she sat on the presidential staff.

What is the difference between Clinton and the Titanic? Only 532 women went down on the Titanic.

Poll of American women asked if they had a chance would they sleep with Clinton. 32% said No once was enough.

What is the difference between a blonde and a mosquito? A mosquito stops sucking when you slap it.

Clinton is in a staff meeting addressing upcoming priorities. His aid says "The Defense bill?" He says " Push it through congress, the republicans will like it." The aid says "The Transportation bill?" Clinton says, "Hold on to that one we have to adjust it." The aid says "The Abortion bill?" Clinton says "What another? Just pay the damn thing!"

Why don't blondes like vibrators? It wrecks their teeth.

Two Newfies drowned when the pick up they were riding in the box of went into the water and they couldn't get the tailgate down.

23 Newfies drowned. Riverdance.

Monica Lewinski's underwear? President's choice.

Difference between a pizza and a pilot? Pizza will feed a family.

Do you love me because I got my money from my family? Don't be silly it doesn't matter where you got the money.

What you get on SAT? Drool

Difference between a wife and a job? Job still sucks after 10 years.

Granny was arrested for having knitting needles on an airplane. She tried to make an afghan

Newfies celebrate yelling 47 days -puzzle said 3 - 5 years.

Newfie cops surrounded store - heard bed linen was on 2 floor

Guy with wooden eye asks deformed girl to dance "Would you like to dance?" "Would I?" She says with enthusiasm. He takes it the wrong way and says "harelip!"

Have you ever got mixed up? I said to the buxom ticket agent "2 Pickets to titsburg."
"that's OK" says other guy " I meant to say to my wife please pass post toasties but instead said - you ruined my life you bitch."

"Mother superior we have discovered a case of syphilis in the convent." "Oh wonderful I was getting tired of the Chablis."

2 silk worms race - end up in a tie.

Gorilla has big fingers because he has big nostrils.

After sex chicken smokes egg upset. I guess we answered that question.

He is so dense light bends around him.

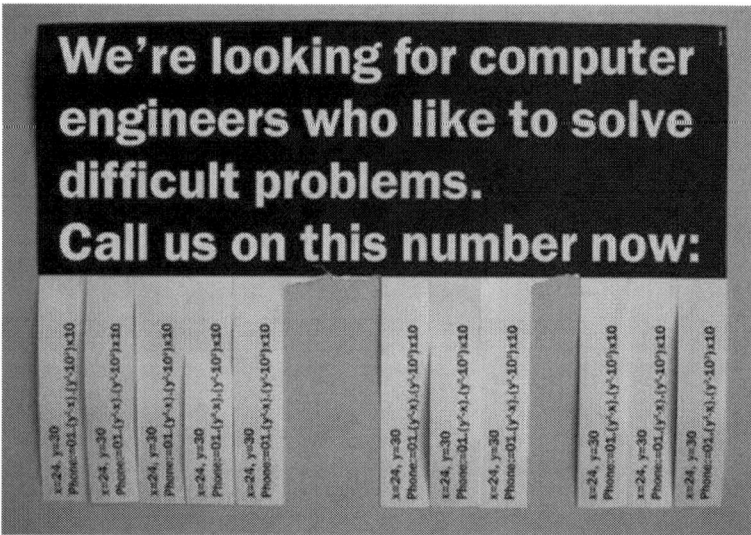

**We're looking for computer engineers who like to solve difficult problems.
Call us on this number now:**

x=24, y=30 Phone=01.(y-x).(y-10)x10

Queen's horse farts while she visits the stables with a Newfie. "I'm sorry." She says. "That's ok" Newfie replies, "I thought it was the horse."

Guy sits beside other at restaurant who passes him the last bowl of chili "You want it I don't." He eats half of it until he finds a dead mouse. He vomits it back into bowl. "That is as far as I got too."

Dyslexic devil worshiper sold soul to Santa

How many lawyers to shingle a roof depends how thin you slice them

New challenging computer game with mystery and graphics -It is called Windows 98

Economists have predicted last 9 out of 5 recessions.

A piece of string who is twisted and ragged is asked if he is a piece of string "nope, I'm a frayed knot."

2 seals walk into a club.

Bartender asks horse why the long face?

Genie gives bottle of booze that never runs dry to Newfie. 2 other wishes. Give me 2 more like this one.

Recall of 2002 Ford Mercury-traces of tuna in them.

Lawyer asks doctor on stand -"Was he breathing?"
No. says the doctor
How did you know he was dead?
His brain was in a jar on my desk but he could be out practicing law somewhere

Irish light bulb 15. 1 to hold the bulb and the rest to drink whiskey until the room spins

Chicken says "book" frog says "readit"

Deep hole. No sound throw rock. Throw in a railroad tie. goat runs into hole farmer looks for goat. No wasn't my goat -It was tied to a railroad tie.

Bartender Dick makes a hickory daiquiri for a surgeon who wants an almond daiquiri.
"Is this an almond daiquiri Dick?"
"No, it's a hickory daiquiri Doc."

Doctor says God must be doc because he made woman out of rib.
Engineer made earth out of chaos.
Lawyer says So who made chaos?

-Kid keeps getting fish ice fishing. When asked how he does it he spits into his hand and says "You have to keep your worms warm."

-God was a civil engineer - who else would run a waste disposal pipeline through a recreational area

Difference between government bonds and men? - Bonds mature.

When I grow up I want to be a musician-you can 't have it both ways

Phone down to desk in low class hotel I got a leak in my sink. Go ahead

To God the relationship-million years/dollars= 1 second/penny
"God can I have a penny? Sure just a second."

I saw my fiancé bending over to pick up something off floor. Couldn't resist, made love.
You are not welcome in Baptist church
I don't care - not welcome in grocery store either.

SOMETIMES
you just know when to keep quiet and stare straight ahead

Contest lost no pun in ten did

What did arts grad say to engineer? Do you want fries with that?

Difference between ignorance apathy and ambivalence-I don't know I don't care one way or another

Corduroy pillows are making headlines

What's another word for thesaurus?

If its tourist season why can't we shoot them

Why isn't phonetics spelled within f?

Why do we wash bath towels

100% COTTON
MACHINE WASH WARM, INSIDE OUT, WITH LIKE
COLORS. USE ONLY NON-CHLORINE BLEACH.
TUMBLE DRY MEDIUM. MEDIUM HOT IRON.
DO NOT IRON PRINT!
———————— OR ————————
GIVE IT TO YOUR WIFE
IT'S HER JOB

Braille dots on drive through ATM

Beer nuts $1.69. Deer nuts 2 under a buck

Bear says I'll have a beer and……..… a shooter –
Bartender asks "why the big paws?"

She cries "make me a real woman" He yells "Here iron
this"

Hey we have a new bathroom light. It goes on when I
pee off when finished. She says, "You are peeing in the
refrigerator."

Foul mouthed parrot emerges from time out in freezer
says, "I'll never swear again but what did the chicken
do?"

Newfie sports -budgie jumping, parrot shooting, hen
gliding

FREE TO GOOD HOME

Beautiful 6 mo. old male kitten - orange & caramel tabby, playful, friendly, very affectionate. Ideal for family w/kids.	OR	Handsome 32 yr. old husband - personable, funny, good job, but doesn't like cats. Says he goes or cat goes.

Call Jennifer - ▆▆▆▆▆ - come see both & decide which you'd like.

Rooster says-cock a doodle do, Blonde says any cock will do

What does a cannibal do after he dumps girlfriend? He wipes his ass

I sold a ton of sporting gear to a guy who came to buy a box of tampons "Your weekend is shot why don't you go fishing."

Wear duh fox hat,

Engineer fixes hell. God says he'll sue. Devil says, "Where will you find a lawyer"

Lawyer brains expensive because rare

I put Viagra in my husband's coffee. He got this gleam in his eye and we had great sex. The problem is we are no longer allowed in Tim Hortons

"All these bulls have lots of sex. Why don't we" she says

He says "Yeah but not with the same cow."

-

What's the difference between the Pope and President Clinton? Get down on only one knee when visiting the pope.

What is the difference between a Harley and a Hoover? Where you place the dirt bag!

Two old ladies were outside their nursing home, having a smoke, when it started to rain. Hilda pulled out a condom, cut off the end, put it over her cigarette, and continued smoking. Her friend, Dorothy, inquired, "What's that?"

"A condom. This way my cigarette doesn't get wet," Hilda explained.

"Where did you get it?"

"You can get them at any drugstore."

The next day, Dorothy hobbled herself into the local drugstore and announced to the pharmacist that she wants a box of condoms. The pharmacist obviously embarrassed, looks at her kind of strangely (she is, after all, more than 80 years of age).

"What brand would you prefer?" he asks delicately.

Dorothy replied, "Doesn't matter son, as long as it fits a Camel."

The pharmacist fainted.

A hippie gets on a bus and spies a pretty young nun.
He sits down next to her, and asks her: "Can we have sex?"
No," she replies, "I'm married to God."
She stands up, and gets off at the next stop.
The bus driver, who overheard, turns to the hippie and says:
"I can tell you how to get to have sex with her!"
"Yeah?" says the hippie.
"Yeah!" says the bus driver. "She goes to the cemetery every
Tuesday night at midnight to pray. So all you have to do is
dress up in robe with a hood, put some of that luminous
powder stuff in your beard, and pop up in the cemetery
claiming to be God."
The hippie decides to give it a try, and arrives in the
cemetery dressed as suggested on the next Tuesday night. "I
am God," he declares to the nun, keeping the hood low about
his face. "Have sex with me."
The nun agrees without question, but begs him to restrict
himself to anal sex, as she is desperate not to lose her
virginity.
'God' agrees, and promptly has his wicked way with her. As
he finishes, he jumps up and throws back his hood with a
flourish.
"Ha-ha," he cries. "I am the hippie!"
"Ha-ha," cries the nun. "I am the bus driver! "

"Ancient Chinese Proverbs"

Virginity like bubble, one prick, all gone.
Man who run in front of car get tired.
Man who run behind car get exhausted.
Man with hand in pocket feel cocky all day.
Foolish man give wife grand piano, wise man give wife
upright organ.
Man who walk through airport turnstile sideways going to
Bangkok.
Man with one chopstick go hungry.
Man who scratch ass should not bite fingernails.

Man who eat many prunes get good run for money.

Baseball is wrong: man with four balls cannot walk.

Panties not best thing on earth but next to best thing on earth.

War does not determine who is right, war determine who is left.

Wife who put husband in doghouse soon find him in cat house.

Man who fight with wife all day get no piece at night.

It take many nails to build crib, but one screw to fill it.

Man who drive like hell, bound to get there.

Man who stand on toilet is high on pot.

Man who live in glass house should change clothes in basement.

Man who fish in other man's well often catch crabs.

Man who fart in church sit in own pew.

Crowded elevator smell different to midget.

What is better than winning 6 medals in the Special Olympics? Not being retarded.

The US military recently detained a math teacher in Iraq. He was carrying a protractor and a compass. The US military spokesman said that the Iraqi was in possession of "Weapons of Math Instruction"...

A first grade teacher explains to her class that she is an American. She asks her students to raise their hands if they were American too. Not really knowing why but wanting to be like their teacher, their hands
explode into the air like flashy fireworks. There is, however, one exception. A girl named Kristen has not gone long with the crowd. The teacher asks her why she has decided to be different.

"Because I am not an American."

"Then", asks the teacher, "What are you?"

"I'm a proud Canadian," boasts the little girl.

The teacher is a little perturbed now, her face slightly red. She asks Kristen why she is a Canadian.
"Well, my mom and dad are Canadians, so I'm a Canadian too."
The teacher is now angry. "That's no reason," she says loudly. "What if your mom was a moron, and your dad was a moron. What would you be then?" A pause, and a smile. "Then," says Kristen, "I'd be an American."

I AM CANADIAN!!!

I AM CANADIAN
(clears Throat)
(the Canadian one is actually a commercial and is all true!)

Hey...
I'm not a lumberjack, or a fur trader...
and I don't live in an igloo, or eat blubber, or own a dogsled...
and I don't know Jimmy, Sally or Suzy from Canada,
although I'm certain they're really, really nice.

I have a Prime Minister, not a President.
I speak English & French, NOT American.
and I pronounce it 'ABOUT', NOT 'A BOOT'.

I can proudly sew my country's flag on my backpack.
I believe in peace keeping, NOT policing.
DIVERSITY, NOT assimilation,
AND THAT THE BEAVER IS A TRULY PROUD AND
NOBLE ANIMAL.

A TOQUE IS A HAT, A CHESTERFIELD IS A COUCH,
AND IT IS PRONOUNCED 'ZED' NOT 'ZEE', 'ZED'!
CANADA IS THE SECOND LARGEST LANDMASS!
THE FIRST NATION OF HOCKEY! AND THE BEST PART
OF NORTH AMERICA!

MY NAME IS JOE!! AND I AM CANADIAN!

 I AM ITALIAN

Ciao...
I'm not a construction worker, a brick layer or a school janitor.
I don't live in a basement, or eat pasta every night.
And I don't drive a Camaro.
And I don't know Tony, Rocco or Gino from Woodbridge,
Although I'm certain they're very, very hairy people.

I drink wine...not beer. I don't use utensils for pizza.
I believe in open bars at weddings, not cash.
And it's pronounced ESPRESSO, not EX-PRESSO.

I can proudly fly my country's flag out of my car during the world cup.
Gelato IS ice cream, Biscotti ARE cookies,
Antonio Columbro IS the best of the tenors,
And it's Broo-SKetta, not Broo-SHetta!

Italy is the ONLY country shaped like footwear,
The FIRST nation of soccer, And the BEST part of Europe!!
My name is Guiseppe !
AND I AM ITALIAN!

I AM PAKISTANI

Allo,
I'm not a cab driver, a 7-11 clerk or a gas attendant.
I don't go to flea markets, or worship elephants, or eat with my hands.
And I don't know Akbar, Rampreet or Mohammed from Rundle,
Although I'm certain they're very smelly people.

I eat roti....not pita. I don't only shower once a week,
I believe in discounts, not full price.
And I pronounce it WHAT, not VHAT.
I can proudly fly my country's flag out of my car during a
terrorist siege.

A turban IS an article of clothing.
 Spicy foods ARE better than mild foods
Curry is a VERY tasty dish,
and it IS pronounced Gaun-dee,not Gun-dee ,GAUN-dee!!

Pakistan IS a third world country,
The first nation of Cricket
And the BEST part of the Middle East!!
My name is Raheem!
>AND I AM PAKISTANI!

INNER BEAUTY
You better have a shitload of it

I AM CHINESE!

Wai...
I'm not a cook, or a computer tech, or the owner of a
laundromat.
I don't live with my parents, I don't eat dog. I don't drive a
souped-up
Civic.
And I don't know Ping, Ching or Wing from Beddington
Heights
Although I'm certain they're very rice... I mean nice people.

I use chopsticks, not a fork. I rarely drive on the sidewalk.
I believe in giving cash, not gifts
And I pronounce it HELLO, not HARRO.
I can proudly wave my country's flag at a tank during a
massacre,

Dim sum IS brunch, Gwai-Los ARE white folk
Jet Li can kick Van Damme's ass any day.
And it IS pronounced Gon Hay Fa Choi, not Gon HEE Fa

China is the LARGEST country in Asia
The FIRST nation of PING-PONG,
And the BEST remaining COMMUNIST COUNTRY!!
My name is FUNG!
AND I AM CHINESE!

and finally........

I AM AMERICAN

Wassup...
I'm not particularly intelligent, open-minded, or well-liked.
And I don't live in a safe place, eat a balanced diet, or drive
very ell.
I don't know Shakespeare, Da Vinci or Gutenberg,

—

although I'm pretty sure they were American.

I drink beer, not water, I am outspoken, not opinionated,
Guns settle disputes, not discussions.
Winning isn't everything, it's the ONLY thing,
And it's pronounced RUFF, not ROOF.

I can proudly sew my country's flag on my backpack, unless I
go somewhere.
Burger King IS fine dining. Washing after peeing is for
LOSERS,
Twinkies and Moon Pies ARE GOOD for breakfast,
I have a SHED, NOT a GARAGE, and WWF ACTION IS
REAL!

The UNITED STATES OF AMERICA is the ONLY country in
the world,
The FIRST nation of IGNORANCE,
And the BEST part of SOUTH AMERICA!!
MY NAME IS JIM-BOB, I am married to my sister,
AND I AM AMERICAN!

There was a city cop on his horse waiting to cross the street
when a little boy on his new shiny bike stopped beside him.
"Nice bike," the cop said. "Did Santa bring it to you?"
"Yep," the little boy said, "he sure did!"
The cop looked the bike over and handed the boy a $20 ticket
for a safety violation. The cop said, "Next year tell Santa to put
a reflector light on the back of it."
The young boy looked up at the cop and said, "Nice horse you
got there sir, did Santa bring it to you?"
"Yes, he sure did," chuckled the cop.
The little boy looked up at the cop and said, "Next year tell
Santa the dick goes underneath the horse, not on top."

TWINS

Because four tits are better than two.

Police station toilet stolen. The cops have nothing to go on.

I dreamt I slept with a muffler around my neck and I woke up exhausted

A flight attendant was stationed at the departure gate to check tickets .As a man approached, she extended her hand for the ticket, and he opened his trench coat and flashed her. Without missing a beat she said, "Sir, I need to see your ticket, not your stub."

Snappy Answer #2
A lady was picking through the frozen turkeys at the grocery store, but couldn't find one big enough for her family. She asked a stock boy, "Do these turkeys get any bigger?" The stock boy replied, "No ma'am, they're dead."

Snappy Answer #3
The cop got out of his car and the kid who was stopped for speeding rolled down his window. "I've been waiting for you all day," the cop said. The kid replied, "Yeah, well I got here as fast as I could." When the cop finally stopped laughing, he sent the kid on his way without a ticket.

Snappy Answer #4
A truck driver was driving along on the freeway. A sign comes up that reads 'Low bridge ahead.' Before he knows it the bridge is right ahead of him and he gets stuck under the bridge. Cars are backed up for miles. Finally, a police car comes up. The cop gets out of his car and walks around to the truck driver, puts his hands on his hips and says, "Got stuck, huh?" The truck driver says, "No, I was delivering this bridge and ran out of gas."

And finally #5 The teacher snappy answer
A college teacher reminds her class of tomorrow's final exam. "Now class, I won't tolerate any excuses for you not being here tomorrow. I might consider a nuclear attack or a serious personal injury or illness, or a death in your immediate family, but that's it, no other excuses whatsoever!" A clown in the back of the room raised his hand and asks, "What would you say if tomorrow I said I was suffering from complete and utter

sexual exhaustion?" The entire class does its best to stifle their laughter and snickering. When silence is restored, the teacher smiles sympathetically at the student, shakes her head, and sweetly says, "Well, I guess you'd have to write the exam with your other hand."

Listening to a whiner?
Call the Wah bulance!

1. NAMES

If Laurie, Linda, Elizabeth and Barbara go out for lunch, they will call each other Laurie, Linda, Elizabeth and Barbara.

If Mark, Chris, Eric and Tom go out, they will affectionately refer to each other as Fat Boy, Godzilla, Peanut-Head and Scrappy.

2. EATING OUT

When the bill arrives, Mark, Chris, Eric and Tom will each throw in $20, even though it's only for $32.50. None of them will have anything smaller and none will actually admit they want change back. When the girls get their bill, out come the pocket calculators.

3. MONEY

A man will pay $2 for a $1 item he needs.

A woman will pay $1 for a $2 item that she doesn't need but it's on sale.

4. BATHROOMS

A man has five items in his bathroom: a toothbrush, shaving cream, razor, a bar of soap, and a towel from the Marriott. The average number of items in the typical woman's bathroom is 337.

A man would not be able to identify most of these items.

5. ARGUMENTS

A woman has the last word in any argument.

Anything a man says after that is the beginning of a new argument.

6. CATS

Women love cats.

Men say they love cats, but when women aren't looking, men kick cats.

7. FUTURE

A woman worries about the future until she gets a husband.

A man never worries about the future until he gets a wife.

8. SUCCESS

A successful man is one who makes more money than his wife can spend.

A successful woman is one who can find such a man.

9. MARRIAGE
A woman marries a man expecting he will change, but he doesn't.

A man marries a woman expecting that she won't change and she does.

10. DRESSING UP
A woman will dress up to go shopping, water the plants, empty the garbage, answer the phone, read a book, and get the mail.

A man will dress up for weddings and funerals.

11. NATURAL
Men wake up as good-looking as they went to bed.

Women somehow deteriorate during the night.

12. OFFSPRING
Ah, children.

A woman knows all about her children. She knows about dentist appointments and romances, best friends, favorite foods, secret fears and hopes and dreams.

A man is vaguely aware of some short people living in the house.

13. THOUGHT FOR THE DAY
Any married man should forget his mistakes. There's no use in two people remembering the same thing.

AND FINALLY.....

A couple drove down a country road for several miles, not saying a word. An earlier discussion had led to an argument and neither of them wanted to concede their position. As they passed a barnyard of mules, jack
asses, and pigs, the husband asked sarcastically, "Relatives of yours?"

"Yep," the wife replied, "in-laws"

BALLS

THEY AREN'T GOING TO SUCK THEMSELVES, LADY

A couple who have been married forever are sitting on the porch one night. Suddenly, the woman reaches over and smacks her husband, knocking him off the porch and into the bushes. He crawls back up and asks, "What was that for?" She says, "For having a little penis." He sits there quietly a moment, and then
smacks her, sending her off the other side of the porch and into the bushes. She crawls back and says, "What was that for?" He says, "For knowing there was more than one size.

1. Now that food has replaced sex in my life, I can't even get into my own pants.

2. Marriage changes passion. Suddenly you're in bed with a relative.

3. I saw a woman wearing a sweatshirt with "Guess" on it. So I said "Implants?" She hit me.

4. I don't do drugs. I get the same effect just standing up fast.

5. Sign in a Chinese Pet Store: "Buy one dog, get one flea..."

6. I live in my own little world. But it's OK. They know me here.

7. I got a sweater for Christmas. I really wanted a screamer or a moaner.

8. If flying is so safe, why do they call the airport the terminal?

9. I don't approve of political jokes. I've seen too many of them get elected.

10. I love being married. It's so great to find that one special person you want to annoy for the rest of your life.

11. I am a nobody, and nobody is perfect; therefore, I am perfect.

12. Everyday I beat my own previous record for number of consecutive days I've stayed alive.
13. How come they choose from just two people to run for president and 50 for Miss America?
15. Isn't having a smoking section in a restaurant like having a peeing section in a swimming pool?
16. Why is it that most nudists are people you don't want to see naked?
17. Snowmen fall from Heaven unassembled.
 18. Every time I walk into a singles bar I can hear Mom's wise words "Don't pick that up, you don't know where it's been!"

A cardiologist died and was given an elaborate funeral. A huge heart covered in flowers stood behind the casket during the service. Following the eulogy, the heart opened, and the casket rolled inside. The heart
then closed, sealing the doctor in the beautiful heart forever. At that point, one of the mourners burst into laughter. When all eyes stared at him, he said, "I'm sorry, I was just thinking of my own funeralI'm a gynecologist." That's when the proctologist fainted.

Those who jump off a bridge in Paris are in Seine.
A backward poet writes inverse.
A man's home is his castle, in a manor of speaking.
Dijon vu - the same mustard as before.
Practice safe eating - always use condiments.
Shotgun wedding: A case of wife or death.
A man needs a mistress just to break the monogamy.
A hangover is the wrath of grapes.
Does the name Pavlov ring a bell?
Condoms should be used on every conceivable occasion.
Reading while sunbathing makes you well red.
When two egotists meet, it's an I for an I.
A bicycle can't stand on its own because it is two tired.
What's the definition of a will? (It's a dead giveaway.)

Time flies like an arrow. Fruit flies like a banana.
In democracy your vote counts. In feudalism your count
votes.
She was engaged to a boyfriend with a wooden leg but broke
it off.

A chicken crossing the road is poultry in motion.
If you don't pay your exorcist, you get repossessed.
With her marriage, she got a new name and a dress.
When a clock is hungry, it goes back four seconds.
The man who fell into an upholstery machine is fully recovered.
You feel stuck with your debt if you can't budge it.
Local Area Network in Australia: the LAN down under.
He often broke into song because he couldn't find the key.
Every calendar's days are numbered.
A lot of money is tainted - It taint yours and it taint mine.
A boiled egg in the morning is hard to beat.
He had a photographic memory that was never developed.
A plateau is a high form of flattery.
A midget fortune-teller who escapes from prison is a small medium at large.
Those who get too big for their britches will be exposed in the end.
Once you've seen one shopping centre, you've seen a mall.
Bakers trade bread recipes on a knead-to-know basis.
Santa's helpers are subordinate clauses.
Acupuncture is a jab well done.

25 Rules of the Air
(from Australian Aviation magazine-June 2000)

1. Every takeoff is optional. Every landing is mandatory.
2. If you push the stick forward, the houses get bigger. If you pull the stick back, they get smaller. That is, unless you keep pulling the stick all the way back, then they get bigger again.
3. Flying isn't dangerous. Crashing is what's dangerous.
4. It's always better to be down here wishing you were up there, than up there wishing you were down here.
5. The only time you have too much fuel is when you're on fire.

6. The propeller is just a big fan in front of the plane, used to keep the pilot cool. When it stops, you can actually watch the pilot start sweating.

7. When in doubt, hold on to your altitude. No one has ever collided with the sky.

8. A 'good' landing is one from which you can walk away. A 'great' landing is one after which you can use the plane again.

9. Learn from the mistakes of others. You won't live long enough to make all of them yourself.

10. You know you've landed with the wheels up if it takes full power to taxi to the ramp.

11. The probability of survival is inversely proportional to the angle of arrival. (Large angle of arrival, small probability of survival, and vice-versa.)

12. Never let an aircraft take you somewhere your brain didn't get to five minutes earlier.

13. Stay out of clouds. The silver lining everyone keeps talking about might be another airplane going in the opposite direction. Reliable sources also report that mountains have been known to hide out in clouds.

14. Always try to keep the number of landings you make equal to the number of takeoffs you've made.

15. There are three simple rules for making a smooth landing. Unfortunately, no one knows what they are.

16. You start with a bag full of luck and an empty bag of experience. The trick is to fill the bag of experience before you empty the bag of luck.

17. Helicopters can't fly; they're just so ugly the earth repels them.

18. If all you can see out of the window is ground that's going round and round, and all you can hear is commotion coming from the passenger compartment, things are not at all as they should be.

19. In the ongoing battle between objects made of aluminum going hundreds of miles per hour and the ground going zero miles per hour, the ground has yet to lose.

---

20.   Good judgment comes from experience. Unfortunately, the experience usually comes from bad judgment.

21.   It's always a good idea to keep the pointy end going forward as much as possible.

22.   Keep looking around. There's always something you've missed.

23.   Remember, gravity is not just a good idea. It's the law. And it's not subject to repeal!

24.   The three most useless things to a pilot are the altitude above you, the runway behind you, and a second ago.

25 SIGNS THAT YOU'VE GROWN UP

1. Your house plants are alive, and you can't smoke any of them.

2. Having sex in a twin bed is out of the question.

3. You keep more food than beer in the fridge.

4. 6:00 AM is when you get up, not when you go to bed.

5. You hear your favourite song on an elevator.

6. You watch the Weather Channel.

7. Your friends marry and divorce instead of hook up and break up.
8. You go from 130 days of vacation time to 14.
9. Jeans and a sweater no longer qualify as "dressed up."
10. You're the one calling the police because those damn kids next door won't turn down the stereo.
11. Older relatives feel comfortable telling sex jokes around you.
12. You don't know what time Taco Bell closes anymore.
13. Your car insurance goes down and your payments go up.
14. You feed your dog Science Diet instead of McDonald's leftovers.
15. Sleeping on the couch makes your back hurt.
16. You no longer take naps from noon to 6 PM.
17. Dinner and a movie is the whole date instead of the beginning of one.
18. Eating a basket of chicken wings at 3 AM would severely upset rather than settle your stomach.
19. You go to the drug store for ibuprofen and antacid, not condoms and pregnancy tests.
20. A $4.00 bottle of wine is no longer "pretty good stuff."
21. You actually eat breakfast food at breakfast time.
22. "I just can't drink the way I used to," replaces, "I'm never going to drink that much again."
23. 90% of the time you spend in front of a computer is for real work.
24. You drink at home to save money before going to a bar.
25. You read this entire list looking desperately for just one sign that doesn't apply to you..........and can't find a single one.

These are entries to a contest asking for a rhyme
with the most romantic first line but ...
the least romantic second line:

Love may be beautiful, love may be bliss
but I only slept with you because I was pissed.

I thought that I could love no other
Until, that is, I met your brother.

Roses are red, violets are blue, sugar is sweet, and so are you.
But the roses are wilting, the violets are dead, the sugar bowl's
empty and so is your head.

Of loving beauty you float with grace
If only you could hide your face

Kind, intelligent, loving and hot;
This describes everything you are not

I want to feel your sweet embrace
But don't take that paper bag off of your face

I love your smile, your face, and your eyes-
Damn, I'm good at telling lies!

My darling, my lover, my beautiful wife:
Marrying you screwed up my life

I see your face when I am dreaming.
That's why I always wake up screaming

My love, you take my breath away.
What have you stepped in to smell this way

My feelings for you no words can tell,
Except for maybe "go to hell"

What inspired this amorous rhyme?
Two parts vodka, one part lime

The following is a telephone exchange between a hotel guest and room service at a hotel in Asia, which was recorded and published in the Far East Economic Review....

Room Service (RS): "Morny. Ruin sorbees."
Guest (G): "Sorry, I thought I dialed room service."
RS: "Rye..Ruin sorbees..morny! Djewish to odor sunteen?"
G: "Uh..yes..I'd like some bacon and eggs."
RS: "Ow July den?"
G: "What?"
RS: "Ow July den?...pry, boy, pooch?"
G : "Oh, the eggs! How do I like them? Sorry, scrambled please."
RS: "Ow July dee bayhcem...crease?"
G: "Crisp will be fine."
RS : "Hokay. An San tos?"
G: "What?"
RS: "San tos. July San tos?"
G: "I don't think so."
RS: "No? Judo one toes??"
G: "I feel really bad about this, but I don't know what 'judo one toes' means."
RS: "Toes! Toes!...Why djew Don Juan toes? Ow bow singlish mopping we bother?"
G: "English muffin!! I've got it! You were saying 'Toast.' Fine. Yes, an English muffin will be fine."
RS: "We bother?"
G: "No..just put the bother on the side."
RS: "Wad?"
G: "I mean butter...just put it on the side."
RS: "Copy?"
G: "Sorry?"
RS: "Copy...tea...mill?"
G: "Yes. Coffee please, and that's all."

RS: "One Minnie. Ass ruin torino fee, strangle ache, crease baychem, tossy singlish mopping we bother honey sigh, and copy....rye??"
G: "Whatever you say"
RS: "Tendjewberrymud."
G : "You're welcome

Two guys sit behind some nuns at a ball game and can't see because of the headgear. To try to get the nuns to move one says, "I think I will move to Montana because there are only 200 nuns in the whole state."
"Naw I'm going to Utah. There are maybe 50 there - tops" says the other
One nun turns around and says, "Why don't you go to hell - there are no nuns there."

Don't marry a woman with large hands- your dick will look small

A father watched his kid inhale six candy bars at a sitting. He says, "Grandpa lived to 107. He didn't eat 6 chocolate bars a day." The kid replies "No, but he did mind his own business."

Time wounds all heels

Two 4 year olds talking about operations. The tonsillectomy is good. You get ice cream and jello afterwards. From his experience at birth the circumcision is bad. You can't walk for year.

Monkey signs to cop after traffic accident. The teenagers drink, smoke and have sex while he drives.

Blonde has an operation. Asks the doctor about recovery time before she can resume her sex life. He says usually 2-3 weeks to recover after a tonsillectomy

Iraq's weather forecast:
  Mostly Sunni for today
  Turning to Shiite tomorrow

"It's easy to explain away anything." says one farmer.
"I don't think so" says the other. "I was trying milk Bessie the
stubborn old cow the other morning. I got down ready and
she whacks me with her tail so I tie it up out of the way to her
horns. I go to sit on the milking stool and she steps on my
foot. So I get some rope and tie that foot to the edge of the
stall. I go to milk her from the other side and she steps on my
toe with her other foot. So I tie that one off. Dag nabbit I had
too much coffee that morning so I take a whiz. I'm just putting
my self back into my pants when my wife comes in and sees
the cow tied up and me hanging onto my dink. Try explaining
that away."

WORK
You're not getting any done now.

Guy says:" What would you do if you caught a man in bed with your wife?"
Other guy says:" First I would break his cane then I would shoot his dog."

Below are actual error messages seen on computer screens in Japan; some are written in Haiku (5,7,5 syllables). Aren't these better than "your computer has performed an illegal operation"?

The Web site you seek cannot be located, but countless more exist.
Chaos reigns within. Reflect, repent, and reboot. Order shall return.
Program aborting: Close all that you have worked on. You ask far too much.

Windows NT crashed. I am the Blue Screen of Death. No one hears your screams.

Yesterday it worked. Today it is not working. Windows is like that.

Our file was so big. It might be very useful. But now it is gone.

Stay the patient course. Of little worth is your ire. The network is down.

A crash reduces your expensive computer to a simple stone.

Three things are certain: Death, taxes and lost data. Guess which has occurred?

You step in the stream, but the water has moved on. This page is not here.

Out of memory. We wish to hold the whole sky, But we never will.

Having been erased, the document you're seeking must now be retyped.

Serious error. All shortcuts have disappeared.

Screen. Mind. Both are blank.

An old hillbilly farmer had a wife who nagged him unmercifully. From morning til night (and sometimes later), she was always complaining about something. The only time he got any relief was when he was out plowing with his old mule. He tried to plow a lot. One day, when he was out plowing, his wife brought him lunch in the field. He drove the old mule into the shade, sat down on a stump, and began to eat his lunch.

Immediately, his wife began haranguing him again. Complain, nag, nag; it just went on and on. All of a sudden, the old mule lashed out with both hind feet; caught her smack in the back of the head. Killed her dead on the spot.

At the funeral several days later, the minister noticed something gather odd. When a woman mourner would approach the old farmer, he would listen for a minute, then nod his head in agreement; but when a man mourner approached him, he would listen for a minute, then shake his head in disagreement. This was so consistent, the minister decided to ask the old farmer about it.

So after the funeral, the minister spoke to the old farmer, and asked him why he nodded his head and agreed with the women, but always shook his head and disagreed with all the men.

The old farmer said, "Well, the women would come up and say some thing about how nice my wife looked, or how pretty her dress was, so I'd nod my head in agreement."

"And what about the men?" the minister asked.

"They wanted to know if the mule was for sale."

ENDINGS
Not everything can end well.

Ever wonder why golf is growing in popularity and why people who don't even play go to tournaments or watch it on TV? The following truisms may shed some light:

Golf is an honourable game, with the overwhelming majority of players being honourable people who don't need referees.

Golfers don't have some of their players in jail every week.

Golfers don't kick dirt on, or throw bottles at, other people.

Professional golfers are paid in direct proportion to how well they play.

Golfers don't get per diem and two seats on a charter flight when they travel between tournaments.

Golfers don't hold out for more money, or demand new contracts, because of another player's deal.

Professional golfers don't demand that the taxpayers pay for the courses on which they play.

When golfers make a mistake, nobody is there to cover for them or back them.

The PGA raises more money for charity in 1 year than the NFL does in 2.

You can watch the best golfers in the world up close, at any tournament, including the majors, all day every day for $25 or $30. The cost for even a nosebleed seat at the Super Bowl costs around $300 or more unless buy it from scalpers in which case it's $1,000+.

You can bring a picnic lunch to the tournament golf course, watch the best in the world and not spend a small fortune on food and drink. Try that at one of the taxpayer funded baseball or football stadiums.

If you bring a soft drink into a ballpark, they'll give you two options get rid of it or leave.

In golf you cannot fail 70% of the time and make $9 million a season, like the best baseball hitters (.300 batting average) do.

Golf doesn't change its rules to attract fans.

Golfers have to adapt to an entirely new playing area each week.

Golfers keep their clothes on while they are being interviewed.

Golf doesn't have free agency

In their prime, Palmer, Norman & other stars, would shake your hand & say they were happy to meet you. In his prime, Jose Canseco wore T-shirts that read "Leave Me Alone."

You can hear birds chirping on the golf course during a tournament.

At a golf tournament, (unlike at taxpayer-funded sports stadiums and arenas) you won't hear a steady stream of four letter words and nasty name calling while you're hoping that no one spills beer on you.

Tiger hits a golf ball over twice as far as Barry Bonds hits a baseball.

Perhaps a smaller ball.

Golf courses don't ruin the neighbourhood.

And finally, here's a little slice of golf history that you might enjoy. Why do golf courses have 18 holes - not 20, or 10, or an even dozen?   During a discussion among the club's membership board at St. Andrews   in 1858, a senior member pointed out that it takes exactly 18 shots to polish off a fifth of Scotch. By limiting himself to only one shot of Scotch per hole, the Scot figured a round of golf was finished when the Scotch ran out...

BOYFRIEND
Next to every hot chick is a guy completely bored
with what he once would kill for.

The FBI' top 12 deaths

Alex Mijtus, 36 years old, is killed by his wife, armed with a 20 inch long vibrator. Mrs Mijtus had enough of her husband's strange sex practices and one night during a prolonged session of fun she snapped, pushing all 20 inches of the vibrator into Alex's anus until it ruptured several vital organs.

 Debby Mills - Newbroughton, 99 years old, was killed as she crossed the road. She was to turn 100 the next day, but crossing the road with her daughter to go to her own birthday party her wheel chair was hit by the truck delivering her birthday cake.

Peter Stone, 42 years old, is murdered by his 8 year old daughter, who he had just sent to her room with no dinner. Young Samantha Stone felt that if she couldn't have dinner no one should, and she promptly inserted 72 rat poison tablets into her father's coffee as he prepared dinner. The victim took one sip and promptly collapsed. Samantha Stone was given a suspended sentence as the judge felt she didn't realize what she was doing, until she tried to poison her mother using the same method one month later.

David Danil, 17 years old, was killed by his girlfriend after he attempted to have his way with her. His unwelcome advance was met with a double-barreled shotgun. Charla's (the girlfriends) father had given it to her an hour before the date started, just in case.

Javier Halos, 27 years old, was killed by his landlord for failing to pay his rent for 8 years. The landlord, Kirk Weston, clubbed the victim to death with a toilet seat after he realized just how long it had been since Mr Halos paid his rent.

Megan Fry, 44 years old, is killed by 14 state troopers after she wandered onto a live firing, fake town simulation. Seeing all the troopers walking slowly down the street Megan Fry had jumped out in front of them and yelled Boo! The troopers, thinking she was a pop up target, fired 67 shots between them, over 40 of them hitting the target. She just looked like a very real looking target, one of the troopers stated in his report.

Julia Smeeth, 20 years old, was killed by her brother Michael because she talked on the phone too long, Michael clubbed his sister to death with a cordless phone, then stabbed her several times with the broken aerial.

Helena Simms, Wife to the famous American nuclear scientist Harold Simms was killed by her husband after she had an affair with the neighbour. Over a period of 3 months Harold substituted Helena's eye shadow with a Uranium composite that was highly radioactive, until she died of radiation poisoning. Although she suffered many symptoms, including total hair loss, welts, blindness, extreme nausea and even had an ear lobe drop off, the victim never attended a doctor's surgery or hospital for a check up.

Conrad Middleton, 26 years old, was killed by his twin brother Brian after a disagreement over who should take the family home after their parents passed away. Conrad had a nasal problem, and had no sense of smell. After the argument Brian stormed out of the house, then snuck back later and turned on the 3 gas taps in the house, filling it with gas. He then left out a box of cigars, a lighter and a note saying, Sorry for the fight, have a puff on me, Brian. Conrad promptly lit a cigar, destroying the house, and himself in the process.

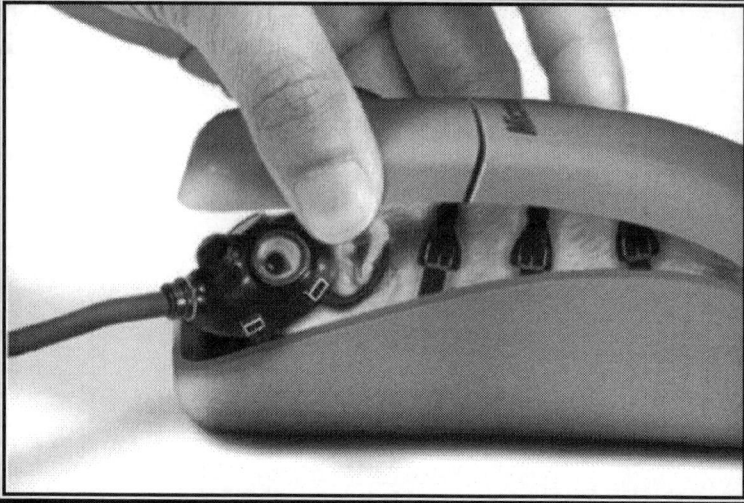

TECHNOLOGY
Easy To Upgrade

Patty Winter, 35 years old, was killed by her neighbour in the early hours of a Sunday morning. Her neighbour, Falt Hame, for years had a mounted F6 phantom jet engine in his rear yard. He would fire the jet engine, aimed at an empty block at the back of his property. Patty Winter would constantly complain to the local sheriff's officers about the noise and the potential risk of fire. Mr Hame was served with a notice to remove the engine immediately. Not liking this he invited Miss Winter over for a cup of coffee and a chat about the whole situation. What Winter didn't know was that he had changed the position of the engine, as she walked into the yard he activated it, hitting her with a blast of 5,000 degrees, killing her instantly, and forever burning her outline into the driveway.

Michael Lewis, angry with his gay boyfriend, used the movie, Die Hard with a Vengeance as inspiration. He drugged his boyfriend, Tony Berry, into an almost catatonic state, then dressed him only in a double sided white board that read Death to all n*ggers! on one side, and God Loves the KKK. on the other. Lewis then drove the victim to downtown Harlem and dropped him off. Two minutes later Berry was deceased.

Military Sergeant John Joe Winter killed his two timing wife by loading her car with Trintynitrate explosive (similar to C4). The Ford Taurus she was driving was filled with 750 kgs of explosive, forming a force twice as powerful as the Oklahoma Bombing. The explosion was heard by several persons some up to 14 kilometres away. No traces of the car or the victim were ever found, only a 55 meter deep crater, and 500m of missing road.

DORMITORY: When you rearrange the letters you get:
DIRTY ROOM

EVANGELIST: When you rearrange the letters:
EVIL'S AGENT

PRESBYTERIAN: When you rearrange the letters:
BEST IN PRAYER

DESPERATION: When you rearrange the letters:
A ROPE ENDS IT

THE MORSE CODE: When you rearrange the letters:
HERE COME DOTS

SLOT MACHINES: When you rearrange the letters:
CASH LOST IN ME

ANIMOSITY: When you rearrange the letters:
IS NO AMITY

MOTHER-IN-LAW: When you rearrange the letters:
WOMAN HITLER

SNOOZE ALARMS: When you rearrange the letters:
ALAS! NO MORE Z'S

A DECIMAL POINT: When you rearrange the letters:
I'M A DOT IN PLACE

THE EARTHQUAKES: When you rearrange the letters:
THAT QUEER SHAKE

ELEVEN PLUS TWO: When you rearrange the letters:
TWELVE PLUS ONE

GEORGE BUSH: When you rearrange the letters:
HE BUGS GORE

And for the grand finale: PRESIDENT CLINTON OF THE
USA: When you rearrange the letters (With no letters left over
and using each letter only once):
TO COPULATE HE FINDS INTERNS

One morning while making breakfast, a man walked
up to his wife, pinched her on the butt and said, "If you
firmed up, we could get rid of your control top panty
hose". While this was on the edge of intolerable, she

kept silent. The next morning, the man woke his wife with a pinch on each of her breasts and said, "You know, if you firmed these up, we could get rid of your bra." This was beyond a silent response, so she rolled over and grabbed him by his tool. With a death grip in place, she said, "You know, if you firmed this up, we could get rid of the gardener, the postman, the poolman, and your brother."

ADOPTION
"Eh, send the little fucker back."

Red Skelton's tips for a happy marriage:

1. Two times a week, we go to a nice restaurant, have a little beverage, then
comes good food and companionship. She goes on Tuesdays, I go on Fridays.
2. We also sleep in separate beds. Hers is in Ontario and mine is in Tucson.
3. I take my wife everywhere, but she keeps finding her way back.

4. I asked my wife where she wanted to go for our anniversary. "Somewhere I haven't been in a long time!" she said. So I suggested the kitchen.
5. We always hold hands. If I let go, she shops.
6. She has an electric blender, electric toaster and electric bread maker.
Then she said "There are too many gadgets and no place to sit down!" So I bought her an electric chair.
7. My wife told me the car wasn't running well because there was water in the carburetor. I asked where the car was, she told me "In the Lake."
8. She got a mudpack and looked great for two days. Then the mud fell off.
9. She ran after the garbage truck, yelling "Am I too late for the garbage?" The driver said "No, jump in!"
10. Remember. Marriage is the number one cause of divorce.
11. Statistically, 100% of all divorces start with marriage.
12. I married Miss Right. I just didn't know her first name was Always.
13. I haven't spoken to my wife in 18 months. I don't like to interrupt her.
14. The last fight was my fault. My wife asked "What's on the TV?" I said "Dust!"

Five surgeons are discussing who makes the best patients to operate on.

The first surgeon says, "I like to see accountants on my operating table because when you open them up, everything inside is numbered."

The second responds, "Yeah, but you should try electricians! Everything inside them is colour coded."

The third surgeon says, "No, I really think librarians are the best; everything inside them is in alphabetical order."

The fourth surgeon chimes in: "You know, I like construction workers. Those guys always understand when you have a few parts left over at the end, and when the job takes longer than you said it would."

But the fifth surgeon shut them all up when he observed: "You're all wrong. Politicians are the easiest to operate on. There's no guts, no heart, no balls, no brains and no spine, and the head and the ass are interchangeable."

A priest and a rabbi are sitting next to each other on an airplane. After a while the priest turns to the rabbi and asks, "Is it still a requirement of your faith that you not eat pork?" The rabbi responds, "Yes, that is still one of our beliefs." The priest then asks, "Have you ever eaten pork?" To which the rabbi replies, "Yes, on one occasion I did succumb to temptation and tasted pork."

The priest nodded in understanding and went on with his reading. A while later, the rabbi spoke up and asked the priest, "Father, is it still a requirement of your church that you remain celibate?" The priest replied, "Yes, that is still very much a part of our faith." The rabbi then asked him, "Father, have you ever fallen to the temptations of the flesh?" The priest replied, "Yes, rabbi, on one occasion I was weak and broke with my faith." The rabbi nodded understandingly. He was silent for about five minutes, and then he said, "Beats the hell out of a ham sandwich, doesn't it?"

A white haired man walked into a jeweler's shop late one Friday, with a beautiful young lady on his side.
"I'm looking for a special ring for my girlfriend," he said.
The jeweler looks through his stock, and takes out an outstanding ring priced at $5,000 "I don't think you understand I want something very unique," he said.
At that, the jeweler went and fetched his special stock from the safe. "Here's one stunning ring at $40,000."
The girls' eyes sparkled, and the man said that he would take it. "How are you paying?" "I'll pay by check, but of course the bank would want to make sure that everything is in order, so I'll write a   check and you can phone the bank tomorrow, then I'll fetch the ring on Monday." Monday morning a very pissed off jeweler phones the man. " You bastard, you lied there's no money in that account." "I know, but can you imagine what a fantastic weekend I had.

A major research institution has recently announced the discovery of the heaviest element yet known to science. The new element has been tentatively named Governmentium. Governmentium has one neutron, 12 assistant neutrons, 75 deputyneutrons, and 11 assistant deputy neutrons, giving it an atomic mass of 312. These 312 particles are held together by forces called morons, which are surrounded by vast quantities of lepton-like particles called peons. Since Governmentium has no electrons, it is inert. However, it can be detected as it impedes every reaction with which it comes into contact. A minute amount of Governmentium causes one reaction to take four days to complete when it would normally take less than a second. Some scientists speculate that Governmentium is formed whenever morons reach a certain quantity in concentration. This hypothetical quantity is referred to as a Critical Morass.When catalysed with money, Governmentium becomes administratium, an element that radiates just as much energy since it has half as many peons but twice as many morons.

A man and a woman, who have never met before, find themselves assigned to the same sleeping room on a transcontinental train. Though initially embarrassed and uneasy over sharing a room, the two are tired and fall asleep quickly...he in the upper bunk and she in the lower.

At 1:00 AM, he leans over and gently wakes the woman saying, "Ma'am, I'm sorry to bother you, but would you be willing to reach into the closet to get me a second blanket? I'm awfully cold."   "I have a better idea," she replies. "Just for tonight, let's pretend that we're married."

"Wow! That's a great idea!!" he exclaims.

"Good," she replies. "Get your own damn blanket!"

After a moment of silence, he farted

Scottish Bar Stool - for when wearing a kilt.....

INTERNET

IT DOESN'T MAKE YOU STUPID, IT JUST MAKES YOUR STUPIDTIY MORE ACCESSIBLE TO OTHERS.

Supervisor Quotes ---These are actual supervisor quotes taken from employee performance evaluations:

1. "Since my last report this employee has reached rock bottom and started to dig."

2. "I would not allow this employee to breed."

3. "This employee is really not much of a has-been, but more of a definite won't be."

4. "Works well when under constant supervision and cornered like a rat in a trap."

5. "When she opens her mouth it seems it is only to change feet."

6. "He would be out of his depth in a parking lot puddle."

7. "This young lady has delusions of adequacy."

8. "He sets low personal standards and then consistently fails to achieve them."

9. "This employee is depriving a village somewhere of an idiot."

10. "This employee should go far, the sooner he starts the better."

11. "Got a full six pack but lacks the plastic thing to hold it all together."

12. "A gross ignoramus --- 144 time worse than an ordinary ignoramus."

13. "He doesn't have ulcers but he is a carrier."

14. "I would like to go hunting with him sometime."

15. "He's been working with glue too much."

16. "He would argue with a signpost."

17. "He brings a lot of joy whenever he leaves the room."

18. "When his IQ reaches 50 he should sell."

19. "If you see two people talking and one looks bored, he is the other one."

20. "A photographic memory but with the lens cap glued on."

21. "A prime candidate for natural de-selection."

22. "Donated his brain to science before he was done using it."

23. "Gates are down, lights are flashing but the train isn't coming."

24. "He's got two brains, one is lost and the other is out looking for it."

25. "If he were any more stupid he'd have to be watered twice a week."

26. "If you gave him a penny for his thoughts you would get change."

27. "If you stand close enough to him you can hear the ocean."

28. "It's hard to believe that he beat out 1,000,000 other sperm."

29. "One neuron short of a synapse."

30. "Some drink from the fountain of knowledge, he only gargled."

31. "It takes him 2 hours to watch 60 Minutes."

32. "The wheel is turning but the hamster is dead."

DICTIONARY FOR WOMEN'S PERSONAL ADS:

40-ish...49

Adventurous.................Slept with everyone

Athletic......................................No tits

Average looking....................Ugly

Beautiful..........................Pathological liar

Contagious Smile..................Does a lot of pills

Emotionally Secure......................On medication

Feminist...Fat

Free spirit.....................................Junkie

Friendship first.........................Former slut

Fun..Annoying

New-Age......Body hair in the wrong places

Old-fashioned.............................No BJs

Open-minded................................Desperate

Outgoing...............Loud and Embarrassing

Passionate...............................Sloppy drunk

Professional....................................Bitch

Voluptuous..................................Very Fat

Large frame...............................Hugely Fat

Wants Soul mate.............................Stalker

RAINBOWS
Not as gay as you might think.

WOMEN'S ENGLISH:

1. Yes = No

2. No = Yes

3. Maybe = No

4. We need = I want..

5. I am sorry = you'll be sorry

6. We need to talk = You're in trouble

7. Sure, go ahead = You better not

8. Do what you want = You will pay for this later

9. I am not upset = Of course I am upset, you moron!

10. You're certainly attentive tonight = Is sex all you ever think about?

MEN'S ENGLISH:

1. I am hungry = I am hungry

2. I am sleepy = I am sleepy

3. I am tired = I am tired

4. Nice dress = Nice cleavage!

5. I love you = Let's have sex now

6. I am bored = Do you want to have sex?

7. May I have this dance? = I'd like to have sex with you

8. Can I call you sometime? = I'd like to have sex with you

9. Do you want to go to a movie? = I'd like to have sex with you

1 0. Can I take you out to dinner? = I'd like to have sex with you

11. I don't think those shoes go with that outfit = I'm gay

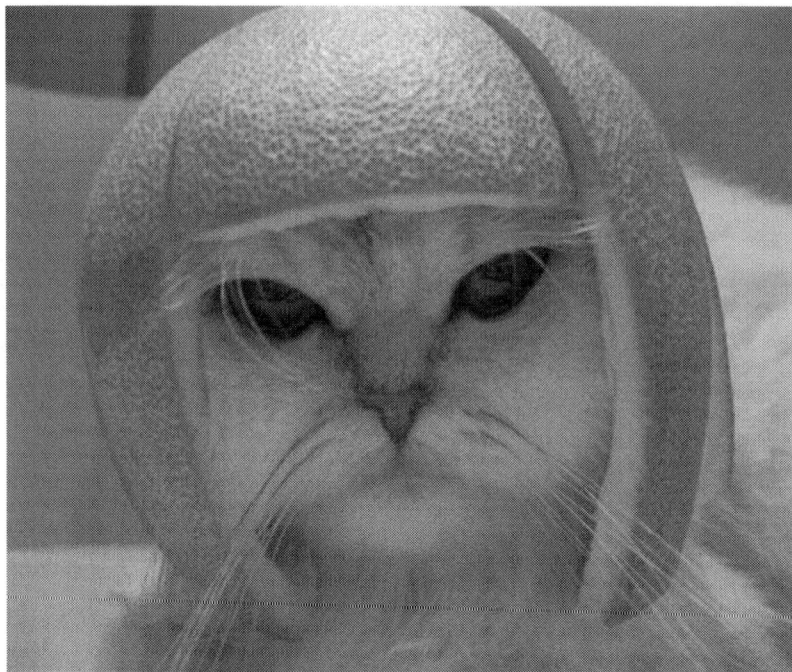

The Lone Ranger and Tonto went camping in the desert. After their tent was all set up, they fell sound asleep. One hour later, Tonto wakes the Lone Ranger and says, "Kemo-Sabe, look towards sky, what you see?" The Lone Ranger replies, "I see millions of stars." "What that tell you?" asked Tonto. The Lone Ranger ponders for a minute, then says, "Astronomically speaking, it tells me there are millions of galaxies and potentially millions of planets. Astrologically, it tells me that Saturn is in Leo. Time wise, it appears to be approximately a quarter past three in the morning. Theologically, it's evident the Lord is all-powerful and we are small and insignificant. Meteorologically, it seems we will have a beautiful day tomorrow. What's it tell you, Tonto?" Tonto is silent for a moment, then says, "Kemo-Sabe, you dumb ass. Someone stole tent."

What do you call an arctic cow?
An eskimoo!

What do you get if you cross a chicken with a cement mixer?
A brick-layer!

Why does a rooster watch TV?
For hentertainment!

What do you call a crate of ducks?
A box of quackers!

The teacher gave her fifth grade class an assignment. Get their parents to tell them a story with a moral at the end of it. The next day the kids came back and one by one began to tell their stories.
Ashley said, "My father's a farmer and we have a lot of egg-laying hens. One time we were taking our eggs
to market in a basket on the front seat of the car when we hit a big bump in the road and all the eggs
went flying and broke and made a mess." "What's the moral of the story?" asked the teacher.
"Don't put all your eggs in one basket!" "Very good," said the teacher. Next little Sarah raised her hand and said, "Our family are farmers too. But we raise chickens for the meat market. We had a dozen eggs one time, but when they hatched we only got ten live chicks, and the moral to this story is, "don't count your chickens before they're hatched." "That was a fine story Sarah. Michael, do you have a story to share?"
"Yes, my daddy told me this story about my Aunt Karen.
Aunt Karen was a flight engineer in the Gulf War and her plane was hit. She had to bail out over enemy territory and all she had was a bottle of whisky, a machine gun and a machete. She drank the whisky on the way down so it wouldn't break and then she landed right in the middle of 100 enemy troops. She killed seventy of them with the machine gun until she ran out of bullets. Then she killed twenty more with the machete until the blade broke. And then she killed
the last ten with her bare hands."

"Good heavens," said the horrified teacher, "what kind of moral did your daddy tell you from that horrible story?" "Stay the f*** away from Aunt Karen when she's been drinking."

A three year old little boy was examining his testicles while taking a bath. "Mama," he asked, "Are these my brains?" Mama answered, "Not yet."

Ten reasons why trick-or-treat is better than sex:
10) You are guaranteed to get at least a little something in the sack.
 9) If you get tired, you can wait 10 minutes and go at it again.
 8) The uglier you look, the easier it is to get some.
 7) You don't have to compliment the person who gives you some.
 6) It's O.K. when the person you're with fantasizes you're someone else, because you are.
 5) Forty years from now you'll still enjoy candy.
 4) If you don't like what you get, you can always go next door.
 3) It doesn't matter if the kids hear you moaning and groaning.
 2) Less guilt the morning after.
 1) You can do the whole neighbourhood.

A Newfie calls up his lawyer and asks. "Wid all them there lawsuits going on, I'm feeling kinda left out . . . how do I get in on some of that action? I hear that people are suing the cigarette companies cause they got cancer, and others are suing the Big Mac company cause they got themselves fat." His lawyer asks, "And which one of those categories do you fit under?" The dear ole Newfie, God bless his soul answers . . . "Neider, I just wanna know if I can sue Labatt's for all the ugly women I've slept with"

---

1. Save the whales. Collect the whole set.
2. A day without sunshine is like night.
3. On the other hand, you have different fingers.
4. I just got lost in thought. It wasn't familiar territory.
5. 42.7% of all statistics are made up on the spot.
6. 99% of lawyers give the rest a bad name.
7. I feel like I'm diagonally parked in a parallel universe.
8. Honk if you love peace and quiet.
9. Remember, half the people you know are below average.
10. He who laughs last thinks slowest.
11. Depression is merely anger without enthusiasm.
12. The early bird may get the worm, but the second mouse gets the cheese.
13 I drive way too fast to worry about cholesterol.
14. Support bacteria. They're the only culture some people have.
15. Monday is an awful way to spend 1/7 of your week.
16. A clear conscience is usually the sign of a bad memory.
17. Change is inevitable, except from vending machines.
18. Get a new car for your spouse. It'll be a great trade!
19. Plan to be spontaneous tomorrow.
20. Always try to be modest, and be proud of it!
21. If you think nobody cares, try missing a couple of payments.
22. How many of you believe in psycho-kinesis? Raise my hand...
23. OK, so what's the speed of dark?
24. How do you tell when you're out of invisible ink?
25. If everything seems to be going well, you have

obviously overlooked something.

26. When everything is coming your way, you're in the wrong lane.

27. Hard work pays off in the future. Laziness pays off now.

28. Everyone has a photographic memory. Some just don't have film.

29. If Barbie is so popular, why do you have to buy her friends?

30. How much deeper would the ocean be without sponges?

31. Eagles may soar, but weasels don't get sucked into jet engines.

32. What happens if you get scared half to death twice?

33. I used to have an open mind but my brains kept falling out.

34. I couldn't repair your brakes, so I made your horn louder.

35. Why do psychics have to ask you for your name?

36. Inside every older person is a younger person wondering what happened.

37. Just remember - if the world didn't suck, we would all fall off.

38. Light travels faster than sound. That is why some people appear bright until you hear them speak.

Dear Abby,

My husband is not happy with my mood swings. The other day, he bought me a mood ring so he would be able to monitor my moods. When I'm in a good mood it turns green. When I'm in a bad mood it leaves a big fucking red mark on his forehead. Maybe next time the asshole will buy me a diamond.

Sincerely,
Bitchy in Ottawa

There was this couple that had been married for 20 years. Every time they made love the husband always insisted on shutting off the light. Well, after 20 years the wife felt this was
ridiculous. She figured she would break him out of this crazy habit.
So one night, while they were in the middle of a wild, screaming, romantic session, she turned on the lights.

She looked down... and saw her husband was holding a battery-operated pleasure device... a vibrator! Soft, wonderful and larger than a real one. She went completely ballistic.

"You impotent bastard," She screamed at him, "how could you be lying to me all of these years? You better explain yourself!"

The husband looks her straight in the eyes and says calmly "I'll explain the toy . . . you explain the kids."

A big Texan cowboy stopped at a local restaurant following a day of drinking and roaming around in Mexico. While sipping his tequila, he noticed a sizzling, scrumptious looking platter being served at the next table. Not only did it look good, the smell was wonderful. He asked the waiter, "What is that you just served?" The waiter replied, "Ah senor, you have excellent taste! Those are bull's testicles from the bullfight this morning. A delicacy!" The cowboy, though momentarily daunted, said, "What the heck, I'm on vacation down here! Bring me an order." The waiter replied, "I am so sorry senor. There is only one serving per day because there is only one bullfight each morning. If you come early tomorrow and place your order, we will be sure to save you this delicacy!" The next morning, the cowboy returned, placed his order, and then that evening he was served the one and only special delicacy of the day. After a few bites, and inspecting the contents of his platter, he called to the waiter and said, "These are delicious, but they are much, much smaller than the ones I saw you serve yesterday!" The waiter shrugged his shoulders and replied, "Si, Senor. Sometimes the bull wins."

A man walked into a supermarket with his zipper down. A lady cashier walked up to him and said, "Your barracks door is open." Not a phrase that men normally use, he went on his way looking a bit puzzled. When he was about done shopping, a man came up and said, "Your fly is open." He zipped up and finished his shopping. At the checkout, he intentionally got in the line where the lady was that told him about his "barracks door." He was planning to have a little fun with her so when he reached the counter he said, "When you saw my barracks door open, did you see a soldier standing in there at attention?" The lady (naturally smarter than the man) thought for a moment and said, "No, no I didn't. All I saw was a disabled veteran sitting on a couple of old duffel bags.

The Washington Post's Style Invitational once again asked readers to take any word from the dictionary, alter it by adding, subtracting, or changing one letter, and supply a new definition. Here are this year's winners:
Bozone (n.): The substance surrounding stupid people that stops bright ideas from penetrating. The bozone layer, unfortunately, shows little sign of breaking down in the near future.
Foreploy (v): Any misrepresentation about yourself for the purpose of getting laid.
Cashtration (n.): The act of buying a house, which renders the subject financially impotent for an indefinite period.
Giraffiti (n): Vandalism spray-painted very, very high.
Sarchasm (n): The gulf between the author of sarcastic wit and the person who doesn't get it.
Inoculatte (v): To take coffee intravenously when you are running late.
Hipatitis (n): Terminal coolness.
Osteopornosis (n): A degenerate disease.
Karmageddon (n): It's like, when everybody is sending off all these really bad vibes, right? And then, like, the

Earth explodes and it's like, a serious bummer.

Decafalon (n.): The grueling event of getting through the day consuming only things that are good for you.

Glibido (v): All talk and no action.

Dopeler effect (n): The tendency of stupid ideas to seem smarter when they come at you rapidly.

Arachnoleptic fit (n.): The frantic dance performed just after you've accidentally walked through a spider web.

Beelzebug (n.): Satan in the form of a mosquito that gets into your bedroom at three in the morning and cannot be cast out.

Caterpallor (n.): The color you turn after finding half a grub in the fruit you're eating.

Ignoranus (n): A person who's both stupid and an asshole.

The sport of choice for the urban poor is BASKETBALL. The sport of choice for maintenance level employees is BOWLING. The sport of choice for front-line workers is FOOTBALL. The sport of choice for supervisors is BASEBALL. The sport of choice for middle management is TENNIS. The sport of choice for corporate officers is GOLF. AMAZING CONCLUSION: The higher you are in the corporate structure, the smaller your balls become.

Why are Redneck murders unsolvable? There are no dental records and all the DNA is the same.

John O'Reilly hoisted his beer and said, "Here's to spending the rest of me life, between the legs of me wife!" That won him the top prize at the pub for the best toast of the night!

He went home and told his wife, Mary, "I won the prize for the best Toast of the night."

She said, "Aye, did ye now. And what was your toast?"

John said, "Here's to spending the rest of me life, sitting in church beside me wife."

"Oh, that is very nice indeed, John!" Mary said.

The next day, Mary ran into one of John's drinking buddies on the street corner. The man chuckled leeringly and said, "John won the prize the other night at the pub with a toast about you, Mary."

She said, "Aye, he told me, and I was a bit surprised meself. You know, he's only been there twice in the last four years. Once he fell asleep, and the other time I had to pull him by the ears to make him come."

What is the difference between a rooster and a hooker?
A rooster clucks defiance. A rooster says cock a doodle doo. A hooker says any cock will do.

A woman gets a labiaedectomy (reduction of vaginal lips) and asks her doctor to keep it a secret. Upon waking up she sees three roses and is furious with the doctor for divulging the secret. "I didn't" the doctor says "One rose is from me, the second from my nurse and the third is from the guy in the burn unit thanking you for the new ears."

A drunken man staggered into a Catholic church, sat down in the Confessional and said nothing. The priest is waiting and waiting and waiting. The priest coughs to attract the drunken man's attention, but still the man says nothing. The priest then knocks on the wall three times in a final attempt to get the man to speak. Finally the drunk replies, "No use knockin,' pal. There's no paper."

SURVIVAL

When you are in deep trouble,
say nothing, and try to look like
you know what you're doing.

Reg Reagan from the footy show has some interesting thoughts on men:

1. If you are over 30 and you have a washboard stomach, you're gay. It means you haven't sucked back enough beer with the boys and rather you've been sucking-off the boys and have spent the rest of your free time doing sit-ups, aerobics, and doing the Oprah diet.

2. If you have a cat, you are a Flaaaayming Fag. A cat is like a dog, but Gay: it grooms itself constantly but never scratches itself, has a delicate touch except when it uses its nails, and whines to be fed. And just think about how you call a dog..."Killer, come here! I said get your ass over here!" Now think about how you call a cat..."Bun-bun, come to daddy, snookums!" Jeeezus, you're the poster boy for GAY.

3. If you suck on lollipops, Ring-Pops, baby-dummies, or any such nonsense, rest assured, you are a Gaylord. A straight

man only sucks bar-b-q ribs, crab-claws, raw oysters, craw-fish guts, pickled pigs feet, or titties. Anything else and you are in training to suck El-Dicko and undeniably a Fag.

4. If you refuse to have a shit in a public toilet or piss in a parking lot, you're in a deep homosexual relationship. A man's world is his toilet; he defecates and urinates where he pleases.

5. If you drink decaf coffee with skim milk, you like a high hard one in the poop-chute. Coffee is to be had strong, black (or with thick, wholesome milk) and full-aroma. A pussy-eating man will never be heard ordering a "Decaf Cafe Latte with Skim" and he will never, ever know what artificial sweetener tastes like. If you've had NutraSweet in your mouth, you've had a dick in there too.

6. If you know more than six names of colours or four different types of dessert, you might as well be handing out a free pass to your arse. A real man doesn't have memory space in his brain to remember all of that crap as well as all the names of all the players in the NRL, Super 12 Rugby, Cricket, PGA, NBL, and Supercar series. If you can pick out chartreuse or you know what a "fresier" is, you're gay. And if you can name ANY type of textile other than denim, you are faggadocious!

7. If you drive with both hands on the wheel, forget it...you're hungry for man sausage. A man only puts both hands on the wheel to honk at slow-arse Volvo drivers or to cut the mother***ker off. The rest of the time he needs that hand to change the radio station, eat his hamburger, hold his beer, or, if he's a wog, talk on his mobile phone.

8. If you enjoy romantic comedies or French films, mon-frere, vous sonnez le Gay, oui? The only time it is acceptable to watch one of those is with a woman who knows how to reward her man. Watching any of the above films by yourself or with another man is likely to result in SHC (spontaneous homosexual combustion), which is what happens to fags

when they flame out too quickly. So follow the rules and beware. Or keep that sh*t to yourself, you flaming faggot!

9. If your name is Ricky, Tom, Stephen or Rob then stop living in denial. You're a dung punching arse bandit from way back and everyone knows it.

There is a new study out about women and how they feel about their bums
85% of women think their ass is too big...
10% of women think their ass is too little...
The other 5% say that they don't care, they love him, he's a good man, and they would have married him anyway.

Camilla Parker Boweles says she is very happy to be getting wed, but says she has turned down the Queen's offer of a free weekend in Paris with car and driver

Wife comes home early from work one day only to find her husband in bed with a strange woman. She says, "That's it, I'm leaving and never coming back." He says, "Don't you at least want to hear my explanation?" She shrugs and says, "Fine, let's hear your story. And this had better be good!"

He says, "Well, I'm driving along the street, when I see this young lady in torn clothes, no shoes, all muddy and crying. I took pity on her and asked if she would like to get cleaned up in my house. She climbed into my truck and I brought her home. She took a shower, I gave her the underwear that doesn't fit you anymore, the silk blouse and slacks that I bought you two years ago that you wore once, the $150 Nike running shoes you bought and wore only twice. I even gave her some of the roast beef you had in the fridge, that you never served me.

I showed her to the door. She was so grateful, for all these things, and she thanked me profusely. But then, as she was about to leave she turned around and asked me........ "Is there anything else your wife
doesn't use anymore?"

One dark night outside a small town in Alberta, a fire started inside the local sausage plant and in a blink it exploded into massive flames. The alarm went out to all the fire departments from miles around. When the volunteer fire fighters appeared on the scene, the sausage company president rushed to the fire chief and said, "All of our secret formulas are in the vault in the center of the plant. They must be saved and I will give $50,000 to the fire department that brings them out intact." But the roaring flames held the firefighters off. Soon more fire departments had to be called in as the situation became desperate. As the firemen arrived, the president shouted out that the offer was now $100,000 to the fire department who could bring out the company's secret files. From the distance, a lone siren was heard as another fire truck came into sight. It was the nearby Mundare rural township volunteer fire department composed mainly of Ukrainians over the age of 65. To everyone's amazement, the little run-down fire engine, operated by these Ukrainians, passed all the newer sleek engines parked outside the plant....and drove straight into the middle of the inferno. Outside the other firemen watched as the Ukrainian old timers jumped off and began to fight the fire with a performance and effort never seen before. Within a short time, the Mundare old timers had extinguished the fire and saved the secret formulas. The grateful sausage company president joyfully announced that for such a superhuman feat he was upping the reward to $200,000, and walked over to personally thank each of the brave, though elderly, Ukrainian firefighters. The local TV news reporters rushed in after capturing the event on film asking, "What are you going to do with all that money?" "Vell," said Nick Sputski, the 70-year-old fire chief, "da furst thing ve gonna do is fix da brakes on dat focking truck!"

A guy goes to the doctor to complain about his penis turning a funny shade of orange. The doctor has never seen anything like this before so he does an ECG, an EKG, a full blood workup and an MRI. He can't figure out what the problem is. An intern chats with the patient and finds out that the guy has recently been laid off and spends his time watching pornos and eating cheezies.

The inventor of the Harley Davidson motorcycle, Arthur Davidson, died and went to heaven. At the gates, St. Peter told Arthur, "Since you've been a good man and your motorcycles have changed the world, your reward is, you can hang out with anyone you want in Heaven."

Arthur thought about it for a minute, and then said, "I want to hang out with God." So St. Peter took Arthur to the throne room and introduced him to God. God recognized Arthur and commented, "Okay, so you were the one who invented the Harley-Davidson motorcycle?"

Arthur said, "Yeah, that's me..."

God commented: "Well, what's the big deal in inventing something that's pretty unstable, makes noise and pollution, and can't run without a road?"

Arthur was apparently embarrassed, but finally spoke. "Excuse me, but aren't you the inventor of woman?"

God replied, "Ah, yes."

"Well," said Arthur, "Professional to Professional, you have some major flaws in your invention:

1. There's too much inconsistency in the front end protrusion.

2. It chatters constantly at high speed.

---

3.   Most of the rear ends are too soft and wobble too much.

4.   The intake is placed way to close to the exhaust.

5.   And the maintenance costs are outrageous"

"HMMMMMMMMMMM, you may have some good points there," replied God, "hold on."God went to his Celestial supercomputer, typed a few words and waited for the results. The computer printed out a slip of paper and God read it. "Well, it may be true that my invention is flawed," God said to Arthur, "but according to these numbers, more men are riding my invention than yours."

Lord, it is these breasts you have given me. The middle one pushes the other two out and I am constantly knocking them with my arms, catching them on branches and snagging them on bushes. "They are a real pain," reported Eve. Eve went on to tell God that since many other parts of her body came in pairs, such as her limbs, eyes, ears, etc......... she felt that having only two breasts might leave her body more "symmetrically balanced," as she put it.
 That is a fair point," replied God, "But it was my first shot at this, you know. I gave the animals six
 breasts, so I figured that you needed only half of those, but I see that you are right. "I will fix it up right
away." And God reached down, removed the middle breast and tossed it into the bushes.
 Three weeks passed and God once again visited Eve in the Garden of Eden.
 Well, Eve, how is my favourite creation?" "Just fantastic," she replied, "But for one oversight on your part". You see, all the animals are paired off. The ewe has a ram and the cow has her bull. All the animals have a mate except me. I feel so alone."

God thought for a moment and said, "You know, Eve, you are right. How could I have overlooked this? You do need a mate and I will immediately create a man from a part of you. Now let's see....... where did I put the useless boob?"

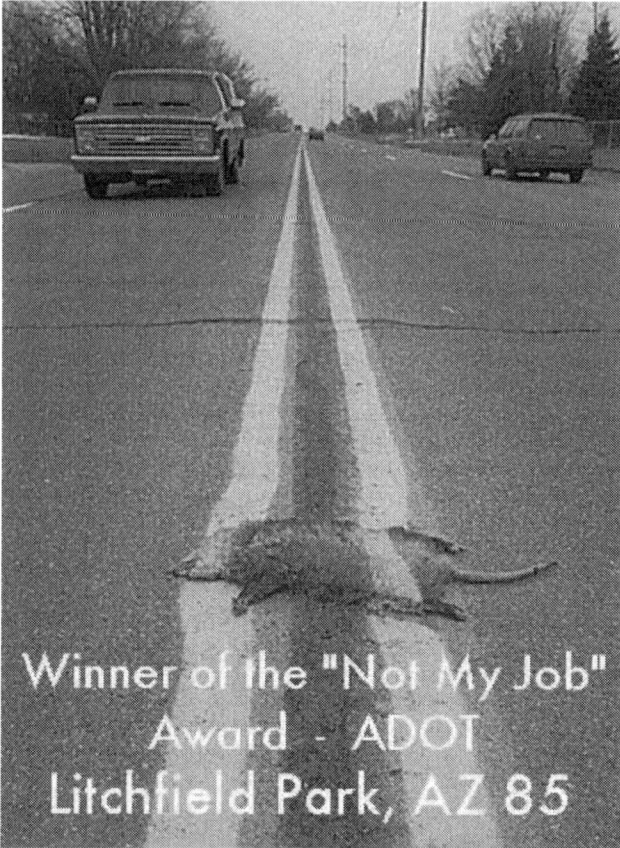

Winner of the "Not My Job"
Award - ADOT
Litchfield Park, AZ 85

A woman stopped by at her recently married son's house. She rang the doorbell and walked in. She was shocked to see her daughter-in-law lying on the couch, totally naked. Soft music was playing, and the aroma of perfume filled the room. "What are you doing?" she asked.

"I'm waiting for my husband to come home from work," the daughter-in-law answered.

"But you're naked!" the mother-in-law exclaimed!

"This is my love dress," the daughter-in-law explained.

"Love dress? But you're naked!"

"My husband loves me to wear this dress," she explained. "It excites him to no end. Every time he sees me in this dress, he instantly becomes romantic and ravages me for hours on end. He can't get enough of me."

The mother-in-law left. When she got home, she undressed, showered, put on her best perfume, dimmed the lights, put on a romantic CD, and laid on the couch waiting for her husband to arrive. Finally, her husband came home. He walked in and saw her laying there so provocatively. "What are you doing?" he asked.

This is my love dress," she whispered, sensually.

Needs ironing," he said. "What's for dinner?"

Man driving DOWN road. Woman driving UP same road. They pass each other.

Woman yells out window, "PIG!".

Man yells out window, "BITCH!".

Man rounds next curve. Crashes into a huge pig in middle of road.

Moral: If only men would listen.

First-year students at Med School were receiving their first anatomy class with a real dead human body. They all gathered around the surgery table with the body covered with a white sheet. The professor started the class by telling them, "In medicine, it is necessary to have 2 important qualities as a doctor. The first is that you not be disgusted by anything involving the human body." For an example, the Professor pulled back the sheet, stuck his finger in the butt of the corpse, withdrew it and stuck his finger in his mouth. "Go ahead and do the same thing," he told his students. The students freaked out, hesitated for several minutes, but eventually took turns sticking a finger in the butt of the dead body and sucking on it. When everyone had finished, the Professor looked at them and told them, "The second most important quality is observation. I stuck in my middle finger and sucked on my index finger. Now learn to pay attention."

After immigrating from Italy two years ago, Sophia goes to the shrink. "Luigi is driving me nuts. He works all the time, picks his nose all the time and always make love in the missionary position." Shrink says, "Let me talk to Luigi."
"Luigi your wife says you are always working, picking your nose and having sex on top. What gives?"
"When I leave for overseas the godfather took me aside and said – Luigi you have to make me proud. When you go to the new world you must work hard, keep your nose clean and above all Luigi, don't fuck up."

A priest was being honoured at his retirement dinner after 25 years in the parish. A leading local politician and member of the congregation was chosen to make the presentation and give a little speech at the dinner. He was delayed so the priest decided to say his own few words while they waited. "I got my first impression of the parish from the first confession I heard here. I thought I had been assigned to a terrible place. The very first person who entered my confessional told me he had stolen a television set and, when stopped by the police, had almost murdered the officer. He had stolen money from his parents, embezzled from his place of business, had an affair with his boss's wife, taken illegal drugs, and gave VD to his sister. I was appalled. But as the days went on I knew that my people were not all like that and I had, indeed, come to a fine parish full of good and loving people." .
Just as the priest finished his talk, the politician arrived full of apologies at being late. He immediately began to make the presentation and give his talk. "I'll never forget the first day our parish priest arrived," said the politician. "In fact, I had the honour of being the first one to go to him to confession."

Mujibar was trying to get into Canada legally through
Immigration. The Officer said, "Mujibar, you have passed
most of the required tests, but there is one more compulsory
test. Unless you pass it you cannot enter Canada." Mujibar
said, "I am ready." The officer said, "Make a sentence using the
words Yellow, Pink and Green." Mujibar thought for a few
minutes and said, "Mister Officer, I am ready." The Officer
said, "Go ahead." Mujibar said, "The telephone goes green,
green, green, and I pink it up, and say, 'Yellow, this is
Mujibar.'" Mujibar now lives in a neighbourhood near you,
and works at a Telus help desk.

There was this guy sunbathing in the nude at the beach. Well, this little girl comes up to him, so he covers his private parts with a newspaper. The little girl says, "What's under there?" So the man answers, "A bird." The girl goes away and afterwards, somehow the man falls asleep. When he wakes up, he found himself in a hospital and in great pain. A doctor comes up to the man and asks him what happened. "I was at the beach and I fell asleep after talking to a little girl." So the doctor tells this to the police, and they go to the beach to find any witnesses. When they get there, they see the little girl the man was talking about. So they ask her if she did anything to the man. She answers, "I didn't do anything to the man, but while he was sleeping, I played with his bird. After a while, it spat at me, so I broke its neck, burnt its nest, and smashed all its eggs!"

What kind of sandals does a frog wear? Open toad.

Honey do these pants make me look fat? No dear, it's your ass that does that.

A 75-year-old man went to his doctor to get a sperm count. The Dr. gave him a jar, sent him home and told him to bring back a semen sample tomorrow. The next day, the 75-year-old man returned to the doctor's office and gave him the jar, which was as clean and empty as on the previous day. The doctor asked what happened, and the man explained, "Well, doc, it's like this. ... First I tried with my right hand, but nothing. Then I tried with my left hand, but still nothing. Then I asked my wife for help. She tried with her right hand, then her left ,still nothing. She even tried with her mouth, first with the teeth in, then with her teeth out, and still nothing. We even called up Arlene, the lady next door, and she tried too, first with both hands, then an armpit, and she even tried squeezing it between her knees, but still nothing." The doctor was shocked. "You asked your neighbour?" The old man replied, "Yep, but no matter what all three of us tried, with our arthritis, we still couldn't get the jar open."

Many years ago in Scotland, a new game was invented. It was ruled "Gentlemen Only...Ladies Forbidden"...and thus the word GOLF entered into the English language.

In the 1400's a law was set forth that a man was not allowed to beat his wife with a stick no thicker than his thumb. Hence we have "the rule of thumb"

The first couple to be shown in bed together on prime time TV were Fred and Wilma Flintstone.

Every day more money is printed for Monopoly than the US Treasury (pre 2009).

Men can read smaller print than women can; women can hear better.

Coca-Cola was originally green.

It is impossible to lick your elbow.

The State with the highest percentage of people who walk to work: Alaska

The percentage of Africa that is wilderness: 28% (now get this...)

The percentage of North America that is wilderness: 38%

The cost of raising a medium-size dog to the age of eleven: $6,400

The average number of people airborne over the US any given hour: 61,000

Intelligent people have more zinc and copper in their hair.

The first novel ever written on a typewriter: Tom Sawyer.

The San Francisco Cable cars are the only mobile National Monuments.

Each king in a deck of playing cards represents a great king from history:

Spades - King David
Hearts - Charlemagne
Clubs -Alexander, the Great
Diamonds - Julius Caesar
111,111,111 x 111,111,111 = 12,345,678,987,654,321

If a statue in the park of a person on a horse has both front legs in the air, the person died in battle. If the horse has one front leg in the air the person died as a result of wounds received in battle. If the horse has all four legs on the ground, the person died of natural causes.

Only two people signed the Declaration of Independence on July 4th, John Hancock and CharlesThomson. Most of the rest signed on August 2, but the last signature wasn't added until 5 years later.

Q. Half of all Americans live within 50 miles of what? A. Their birthplace
Q. Most boat owners name their boats. What is the most popular boat name requested? A. Obsession   Q. If you were to spell out numbers, how far would you have to go until you would find the letter "A"? A. One thousand

Q. What do bulletproof vests, fire escapes, windshield wipers, and laser printers all have in common? A. All invented by women.

Q. What is the only food that doesn't spoil? A. Honey

Q. Which day are there more collect calls than any other day of the year? A. Father's Day

In Shakespeare's time, mattresses were secured on bed frames by ropes. When you pulled on the ropes the mattress tightened, making the bed firmer to sleep on. Hence the phrase......... "goodnight, sleep tight."

WINNERS
BECAUSE NOTHING SAYS "YOU'RE A LOSER" MORE THAN OWNING
A MOTIVATIONAL POSTER ABOUT BEING A WINNER.

It was the accepted practice in Babylon 4,000 years ago that for a month after the wedding, the bride's father would supply his son-in-law with all the mead he could drink. Mead is a honey beer and because their calendar was lunar based, this period was called the honey month. which we know today as the honeymoon.

In English pubs, ale is ordered by pints and quarts... So in old England, when customers got unruly, the bartender would yell at them "Mind your pints and quarts, and settle down." It's where we get the phrase "mind your P's and Q's"

Many years ago in England, pub frequenters had a whistle baked into the rim, or handle, of their ceramic cups. When they needed a refill, they used the whistle to get some service. "Wet your whistle" is the phrase inspired by this practice. At least 75% of people who read this will try to lick their elbow

I cdnuolt blveiee taht I cluod aulaclty uesdnatnrd waht I was rdgnieg.The phaonmneal pweor of the hmuan mnid Aoccdrnig to rscheearch at Cmabrigde Uinervtisy, it deosn't mttaer in waht oredr the ltteers in a wrod are, the olny iprmoatnt tihng is taht the frist and lsat ltteer be in the rghit pclae. The rset can be a taotl mses and you can sitll raed it wouthit a porbelm. Tihs is bcuseae the huamn mnid deos not raed ervey lteter by
istlef, but the wrod as a wlohe. Amzanig huh

The police arrested Ward Branham, a 22-year-old white male, resident of Lethbridge, Alberta, in a pumpkin patch at 11:38 p.m. on Friday. Ward will be charged with lewd and lascivious behaviour, public indecency and public intoxication at the Calgary courthouse on Monday. The suspect explained that as he was passing a pumpkin patch he decided to stop. "You know, a pumpkin is soft and squishy inside, and there was no one around there for miles. At least I thought there wasn't," he stated in a phone interview. Ward went on to say that he pulled over to the side of the road, picked out a pumpkin that he felt was appropriate to his purposes, cut a hole in it, and proceeded to satisfy his alleged "need." "I guess I was just really into it, you know?" he commented with evident embarrassment. In the process, Ward apparently failed to notice a police car approaching and was unaware of his audience until officer Brin Taylor approached him. "It was an unusual situation, that's for sure," said officer Taylor. "I walked up to (Ward) and he's...just working away at this pumpkin. " Taylor went on to describe what happened when SHE approached Ward. "I just went up and said, "Excuse me sir, but do you realize that you are screwing a pumpkin?" He froze and was clearly very surprised that I was there, and then looked me straight in the face and said, ... "A pumpkin? Damn...is it midnight already?"

A man walked into a Tavern and sat next to a very attractive, smartly dressed woman perched on a bar stool. "Hi there, Good Looking. How's it going?" he asked. The woman looked him straight in the eye and said, "Listen, I'll screw anybody, anytime, anywhere, your place, my place, it doesn't matter. I've been doing it ever since I got out of college, and I just love it!" "No kidding?," said the man, "I'm a lawyer too! What firm are you with?"

I checked into a hotel on a business trip and was a bit lonely so I thought I'd get me one of those girls you see advertised in phone booths when you're calling for a cab. I grabbed a card on my way in. It was an ad for a girl calling herself Erogonique, a lovely girl, bending over in the photo. She had all the right curves in all the right places, beautiful long wavy hair, long graceful legs all the way up. You know the kind. So I went to my room and figured, what the heck, I'd give her a call. "Hello?" the woman said. Wow! She sounded sexy. "Hi, I hear you give a great massage and I'd like you to come to my room and give me one. No, wait, I should be straight with you. I'm in town all alone and what I really want is sex. I want it hard, I want it hot, and I want it now. I'll talk kinky the whole night long. You name it, we'll do it. Bring implements, toys, everything you've got in your bag of tricks. We'll go hot and heavy all night; Tie me up, wear a strap on, cover me in chocolate syrup and whipped cream, anything you want baby. Now, how does that sound?" She said, "That sounds interesting. However, for an outside line Sir, you need to press 9."

A bald man with a wooden leg gets invited to a Halloween party. He doesn't know what costume to wear to hide his head and his leg, so he writes to a costume company to explain his problem. A few days later he received a parcel with the following note:
Dear Sir,

Please find enclosed a pirate's costume. The spotted handkerchief will cover your bald head and, with your wooden leg, you will be just right as a pirate.
Very truly yours,
Acme Costume Company

The man thinks this is terrible because they have just emphasized his wooden leg and so he writes a letter of complaint. A week goes by and he receives another parcel and a note, which says:

Dear Sir,
Please find enclosed a monk's habit.
The long robe will cover your wooden leg and, with your bald head, you will really look the part.
Very truly yours,
Acme Costume Company

Now the man is really upset since they have gone from emphasizing his wooden leg to emphasizing his bald head. So again he writes the company another nasty letter of complaint. The next day he gets a small parcel and a note which reads:

Dear Sir,
Please find the enclosed bottle of molasses. Pour the molasses over your bald head, stick your wooden leg up your ass and go as a caramel apple.
Very truly yours,
Acme Costume Company

Jack wakes up at home with a huge hangover he can't believe. He forces himself to open his eyes, and the first thing he sees is a couple of aspirins next to a glass of water on the side table. And, next to them, a single red rose! Jack sits down and sees his clothing in front of him, all clean and pressed. Jack looks around the room and sees that it is in perfect order, spotlessly clean. So is the rest of the house.

He takes the aspirins, cringes when he sees a huge black eye staring back at him in the bathroom mirror, and notices a note on the table: "Honey, breakfast is on the stove, I left early to go shopping--Love you!" He stumbles to the kitchen and sure enough, there is hot breakfast and the morning newspaper. His son is also at the table, eating. Jack asks, "Son...what happened last night?" "Well, you came home after 3 A.M., drunk and out of your mind. You broke some furniture, puked in the hallway, and got that black eye when you ran into the door.""So, why is everything in such perfect order, so clean, I have a rose, and breakfast is on the table waiting for me?" His son replies, "Oh THAT!... Mom dragged you to the bedroom, and when she tried to take your pants off, you screamed, "Leave me alone, lady, I'm married!' "

Broken furniture - $85.26

Hot Breakfast - $4.20

Red Rose bud - $3.00

Two Aspirins - $.38

Saying the right thing, at the right time........Priceless.

Peter met Sharon in a nightclub. They enjoyed each other's company very much and at the end of the evening. Sharon invited Peter to her place, where they quickly got involved in a very passionate and energetic session in bed together.

Finally, tired and satisfied, they both lay back in the bed and snuggled up close to each other. After a short while, Sharon began tenderly stroking Peter's manhood. Surprised but appreciative, Peter comments, "surely you can't be ready for more already?" Sharon replies, "No, but every now and then I get a bit nostalgic and I miss the days when I had my own."

This letter was sent to the principal's office after an elementary school had sponsored a luncheon for the elderly. An old lady had received a new radio at the lunch as a door prize and was writing to say thank you. Dear Faculty and Students:
God bless you for the beautiful radio I won at your recent senior's luncheon. I am 84 years old and live at an Assisted Home for the Aged. All of my family has passed away, and I am all alone now and it's nice to know someone is thinking of me. God bless you for your kindness to an old forgotten lady. My roommate is 95 and always had her own radio. Before I received this one, she would never let me listen to hers, even when she was napping. The other day, her radio fell off the night stand and broke into a lot of little pieces. It was awful and she was in tears. She asked me if she could listen to mine, and I said fuck you.
Thank you for that opportunity. Sincerely, Agnes

A man in a hot air balloon realized he was lost. He reduced altitude and spotted a woman below. He descended a bit more and shouted, "Excuse me, can you help? I promised a friend I would meet him an hour ago, but I don't know where I am." The woman below replied, "You are in a hot air balloon hovering approximately 30 feet above the ground. You are between 40 and 41 degrees North latitude and between 50 and 60 degrees West longitude." "You must be an engineer", said the balloonist. "Indeed, I am", replied the woman. "How did you know?" "Well", answered the balloonist, "everything you told me is technically correct, but I have no idea what to make of your information, and the fact is I am still lost. Frankly, you have not been much help so far." The woman below responded, "You must be in management." "I am", replied the balloonist, "but how did you know?" "Well," said the woman, "you don't know where you are or where you are going. You have risen to where you are due to a large quantity of hot air. You made a promise which you have no idea how to keep, and you expect people beneath you to solve your problems. The fact is, you are exactly in the same position you were in before we met, but now, somehow, it's my fault."

A man walks into a bar and orders a drink. The bar has a robot bartender. The robot serves him a perfectly prepared cocktail, and then asks him, "What's your IQ?" The man replies "150" and the robot proceeds to make conversation about global warming factors, quantum physics and spirituality, biomimicry, environmental interconnectedness, string theory, nano-technology, and sexual proclivities. The customer is very impressed and thinks, "This is really cool." So he decides to test the robot. The next day he goes back to the same bar and orders another drink. Again, the robot serves him the perfectly prepared drink and asks him, "What's your IQ?" The man responds, "about 100."Immediately the robot starts talking, but this time, it talks about hockey, Formula 1 Racing, baseball, supermodels, favourite fast foods, fast cars and women's breasts. Really impressed, the man leaves the bar and decides to test the robot one more time. So the following day he goes back and orders another drink, again the robot serves him a perfect drink and asks, "What's your IQ?" The man replies, "Uhh..dunno... 'round 50... I think..?"and the robot says... really slowly..."So......ya gonna vote for the Liberals again?"

A professor was giving a lecture on "Involuntary Muscular Contractions" to first year medical students.
Realizing that this was not the most riveting subject the professor decided to lighten the mood slightly.
He pointed to a young woman in the front row and said, "Do

you know what your ass hole is doing while you're having an orgasm?" She replied, "He's probably drinking beer at the bar with his friends"

GUTS - is arriving home late, after a night out with the guys, being assaulted by your wife with a broom, and having the guts to ask: "Are you still cleaning, or were you flying off somewhere?"

BALLS - is coming home late after a night out with the guys, smelling of perfume and beer, lipstick on your collar, slapping your wife on the ass and having the balls to say: "You're next."

The husband and wife go to a counselor after 35 years of marriage. The counselor asks them what the problem is and the wife goes into a tirade listing every problem they have ever had in the 35 years they've been married. She goes on and on and on. Finally, the counselor gets up, goes around the desk, embraces the woman and kisses her passionately rips off her clothes and makes mad passionate Love to her. Needless to say, the woman shuts up and sits quietly with a very satisfied daze. The counselor turns to the husband and says "that is what your wife needs At least three times a week. Can you do that?" The husband thinks for a moment and replies, "Well, I can get her here Monday and Wednesday, but Friday I play golf.

A Saskatchewan policeman had a perfect spot to watch for speeders, but wasn't getting many. Then he discovered the problem - a 12-year-old boy was standing up the road with a hand painted sign, which read
"RADAR TRAP AHEAD". The officer then found a young accomplice down the road with a sign reading "TIPS" and a bucket full of money.

A motorist was mailed a picture of his car speeding through an automated radar post in Edmonton AB. A $40 speeding ticket was included. Being cute, he sent the police department a picture of $40. The police
responded with another mailed photo of handcuffs.

A young woman was pulled over for speeding. As the Saskatchewan R.C.M.P. Officer walked to her car window, flipping open his ticket book, she said, "I bet you are going to sell me a ticket to the R.C.M.P. Ball." He replied, "Ma'am, Saskatchewan R.C.M.P. don't have balls." There was a moment of silence while she smiled, and he realized what he'd just said. He then closed his book, got back in his patrol car and drove off. She was laughing too hard to start her car.

At the end of the tax year the Tax Office sent an inspector to audit the books of a synagogue. While he was checking the books he turned to the Rabbi and said, "I notice you buy a lot of candles. What do you do with

the candle drippings? "Good question," noted the Rabbi. "We save them up and send them back to
the candle makers, and every now and then they send us a free box of candles."
"Oh," replied the auditor, somewhat disappointed that his unusual question had a practical answer. But on he went, in his obnoxious way: "What about all these matzo purchases? What do you do with the crumbs?"
"Ah, yes," replied the Rabbi, realizing that the inspector was trying to trap him with an unanswerable question. "We collect them and send them back to the manufacturers, and every now
and then they send a free box of matzo balls."
"I see," replied the auditor, thinking hard about how he could fluster the know-it-all Rabbi. "Well, Rabbi," he went on, "what do you do with all the leftover foreskins from the circumcisions you perform?"
"Here, too, we do not waste, "answered the Rabbi. "What we do is save up all the foreskins and send them to the Tax Office, and about once a year they send us a complete prick."

Two couples were playing poker one evening. John accidentally dropped some cards on the floor. When he bent down to pick them up, he noticed that Bill's wife, Sue, wasn't wearing any underwear under her dress!
Shocked by this, John, upon trying to sit back up again, hit his head on the table and emerged, red-faced.
Later, John went into the kitchen to get some refreshments. Bill's wife followed him and asked "Did you see anything that you liked under there?"
Surprised by her boldness, John courageously admitted that, well, indeed, he had.
She said, "Well you can have it but it will cost you $500.00"

After taking a moment or two to assess the financial and moral costs of this offer, John confirms that he is interested. She tells him that since her husband, Bill works Friday afternoons and as John doesn't, he should come by her hours around 2 p.m.

When Friday rolled around, John showed up at john's house at 2 p.m. sharp and after paying Sue the agreed sum of $500.00 they went to the bedroom and closed their transaction, as agreed. John then quickly dressed and left.
As usual, Bill came home from work at 6 p.m. and upon entering the house, asked his wife abruptly, "Did John come by the house this afternoon?"
With a lump in her throat Sue answered, "Why yes, he did stop for a few minutes this afternoon."
Her heart nearly skipped a beat when her husband curtly asked, "And did he give you $500.00"
In terror, she assumed that somehow he had found out and after mustering her best poker face, replied, "Well, yes, as a matter of fact he did give me $500.00"
Bill, with a satisfied look on his face, surprised his wife by saying, "Good, I was hoping that he did. He stopped by my office this morning and borrowed $500.00 from me. He promised me he'd stop by our house this afternoon on his way and pay me back."
Now, THAT, my friends, is a poker player

As incredible as it sounds, men and women took baths only twice a year (May and October) Women kept their hair covered, while men shaved their heads (because of lice and bugs) and wore wigs. Wealthy men could afford good wigs made from wool. They couldn't wash the wigs, so to clean them they would carve out a loaf of bread, put the wig in the shell, and bake it for 30 minutes. The heat would make the wig big and fluffy, hence the term 'big wig.' Today we often use the term 'here comes the Big Wig' because someone appears to be or is powerful and wealthy.

An elderly man in East Texas had owned a large farm for several years. He had a large pond in the back. It was properly shaped for swimming, so he fixed it up nice -- picnic tables, horseshoe courts, and some apple and peach trees. One evening the old farmer decided to go down to the pond, as he hadn't been there for a while, and look it over. He grabbed a five gallon bucket to bring back some fruit. As he neared the pond, he heard voices shouting and laughing with glee. As he came closer he saw it was a bunch of young women skinny-dipping in his pond. He made the women aware of his presence and they all went to the deep end. One of the women shouted to him, "We're not coming out until you leave!" The old man frowned, "I didn't come down here to watch you ladies swim naked or make you get out of the pond naked." Holding the bucket up he said, "I'm here to feed the alligator."

Moral: Some old men can still think fast.

A man was sitting on the edge of the bed, observing his wife, looking at herself in the mirror. Since her birthday was not far off he asked what she'd like to have for her Birthday. "I'd like to be six again", she replied, still looking in the mirror. On the morning of her Birthday, he arose early, made her a nice big bowl of Lucky Charms, and then took her to Six Flags theme park. What a day! He put her on every ride in the park; the Death Slide, the Wall of Fear, the Screaming Monster Roller Coaster, everything there was. Five hours later they staggered out of the theme park. Her head was reeling and her stomach felt upside down. He then took her to a McDonald's where he ordered her a Happy Meal with extra fries and a chocolate shake. Then it was off to a movie, popcorn, a soda pop, and her favourite candy, M&M's. What a fabulous adventure! Finally she wobbled home with her husband and collapsed into bed exhausted. He leaned over his wife with a big smile and lovingly asked, "Well Dear,

what was it like being six again??"
Her eyes slowly opened and her expression suddenly changed
"I meant my dress size, you dumb dingy"
The moral of the story: Even when a man is listening, he is
going to get it wrong.

Why do we press harder on a remote control when we know
the batteries are getting weak?
Why do banks charge a fee on "insufficient funds" when they
know there is not enough?
Why does someone believe you when you say there are four
billion stars, but check when you say the paint is wet?
Why doesn't glue stick to the bottle?
Why do they use sterilized needles for death by lethal
injection?
Why doesn't Tarzan have a beard?
Why does Superman stop bullets with his chest, but ducks
when you throw a revolver at him?
Why do Kamikaze pilots wear helmets?
Whose idea was it to put an "S" in the word "lisp"?
If people evolved from apes, why are there still apes?
Why is it that no matter what colour bubble bath you use the
bubbles are always white?
Is there ever a day that mattresses are not on sale?
Why do people constantly return to the refrigerator with
hopes that something new to eat will have materialized?
Why do people keep running over a string a dozen times with
their vacuum cleaner, then reach down, pick it up, examine it,
then put it down to give the vacuum one more chance?
Why is it that no plastic bag will open from the end on your
first try?
How do those dead bugs get into those enclosed light
fixtures?
When we are in the supermarket and someone rams our ankle
with a shopping cart then apologizes for doing so, why do we
say, "It's all right?" Well, it isn't all right, so why don't we say,
"That hurt, you stupid idiot?"

Why is it that whenever you attempt to catch something that's falling off the table you always manage to knock something else over?

In winter why do we try to keep the house as warm as it was in summer when we complained about the heat?

How come you never hear father-in-law jokes?

The statistics on sanity are that one out of every four persons is suffering from some sort of mental illness. Think of your three >>best friends -- if they're okay, then it's you.

A drunk man, who smelled like beer, sat down on a subway seat next to a priest. The man's tie was stained, his face was plastered with red lipstick, and a half empty bottle of gin was sticking out of his torn coat pocket. He opened his newspaper and began reading. After a few minutes, the man turned to the priest and asked, "Say Father, what causes arthritis?" The priest replied, "My Son, it's caused by loose living; being with cheap, wicked women; too much alcohol; contempt for your fellow man; sleeping around with prostitutes; and lack of bathing." The drunk muttered in response, "Well, I'll be darned," then returned to his paper. The priest, thinking about what he had said, nudged the man and apologized. "I'm very sorry. I didn't mean to come on so strong. How long have you had arthritis?" The drunk answered, "I don't have it, Father. I was just reading here that the Pope does."

You don't appreciate a lot of stuff in school until you get older. Little things like: being spanked every day by an attractive middle-aged woman. Stuff you pay good money for, later in life."

    Elmo Phillips

" It isn't premarital sex if you have no intention of getting married."

    George Burns

"Having sex is like playing bridge. If you don't have a good

partner, you'd better have a good hand."
Woody Allen

"Bisexuality immediately doubles your chances for a date on Saturday night."
Rodney Dangerfield

"There are a number of mechanical devices which increase sexual arousal, particularly in women. Chief among these is the Mercedes-Benz 380SL."
Lynn Lavner

"Sex at age 90 is like trying to shoot pool with a rope."
Camille Paglia

"Sex is one of the nine reasons for incarnation. The other eight are unimportant."
George Burns

"Women might be able to fake orgasms. But men can fake a whole relationship."
Sharon Stone

"Hockey is a sport for white men. Basketball is a sport for black men. Golf is a sport for white men dressed like black pimps."
Tiger Woods

"My mother never saw the irony in calling me a son-of-a-bitch."
Jack Nicholson

" Clinton lied. A man might forget where he parks or where he lives, but he never forgets oral sex, no matter how bad it is."
Barbara Bush (Former US First Lady, and you didn't think Barbara had a sense of humour)

"Ah, yes, divorce, from the Latin word meaning to rip out a man's genitals through his wallet."
    Robin Williams

"Women need a reason to have sex. Men just need a place."
    Billy Crystal

"According to a new survey, women say they feel more comfortable undressing in front of men than they
 do undressing in front of other women. They say that women are too judgmental, where, of course,
men are just grateful."
    Robert De Niro

"There's a new medical crisis. Doctors are reporting that many men are having allergic reactions to latex
 condoms. They say they cause severe swelling. So what's the problem?"
    Dustin Hoffman

"There's very little advice in men's magazines, because men think, 'I know what I'm doing. Just show me
 somebody naked'."
    Jerry Seinfeld

"See, the problem is that God gives men a brain and a penis, and only enough blood to run one at a time."
    Robin Williams

" It's been so long since I've had sex, I've forgotten who ties up whom."
    Joan Rivers

" Bigamy is having one wife too many. Monogamy is the same."
    Oscar Wilde

A mother is driving her 7 year-old daughter to her friend's house for a play date when the little girl asks "Mommy," how old are you?" "Honey, you are not supposed to ask a lady her age," the mother replies sweetly. "It's not polite." "OK", the little girl says, "How much do you weigh?" "Now really," the mother says, a bit less sweetly. "Those are personal questions and are really none of your business." Undaunted, the little girl asks, "Why did you and Daddy get a divorce?" "That's enough questions, young lady, honestly!" mom says as her daughter is getting out of the car. The exasperated mother drives away as the two friends begin to play. "My Mom won't tell me anything about her," the little girl says to her friend. "Well," says the friend, "all you need to do is look at her drivers license. It's like a report card, it has everything on it." Later that night the little girl says to her mother, "I know how old you are, you are 32." The mother is surprised and asks, "How did you find that out?" "I also know that you weigh 140 pounds." The mother is past surprised and shocked now. "How in heaven's name did you find that out?" "And," the little girl says triumphantly, "I know why you and daddy got a divorce." Now mom's getting mad. She says, "Oh really? And just why is that, young lady?" "Because you got an F in sex."

A black man and his wife were going to a Halloween party in a couple of days so the husband tells his wife to go to the store and get costumes for them to wear. When he comes home that night he goes into the bedroom and there laid out on the bed is a Superman costume. The husband yells at his wife, What are you doing? Have you ever heard of a black Superman? Take this back and get me something else I can wear. The next day the wife, not too happy, returns the costume and gets a replacement. The husband comes home from work goes to the bedroom and there laid out on the bed, is a Batman costume. He again yells at his poor wife, "What are you doing? Have you ever heard of a black Batman? Take this back and get me something I can wear to the costume party!" The next morning his irate wife goes shopping. When the husband comes home again from work, there laid out on the bed are three items one is a set of three white buttons, the second is a thick white belt, and the third item is a 2 x 4 The husband yells at the wife, What the hell are these for? " The wife yells back, " Take your clothes off. You can put the three white buttons on the front of you and go as a domino. If you don't like that idea, you can put the white belt on and go as an Oreo. And if you don't like THAT idea, you can shove the 2 x 4 up your ass and go as a fudgesicle!

There's this theme Halloween party...Everyone has to dress as an emotion.
There's a women dressed from head to toe in green she's Envy. Another guy is dressed all in red...he's anger. Yellow...well, you get the idea.
The door bell rings at the party and the hosts open to door to find a very large, nude black guy standing there with a jello pudding cup strapped to his genital area.
The hosts asked what emotion are you supposed to be? He replied "I'm fuckin' dis custed.

The older trophy wife of a rich man asks for something that goes from 0 to 200 in less than ten seconds for Christmas. He gives her a bathroom scale.

⚠ HAZARDOUS MATERIALS DATA SHEET ☢

ELEMENT:	Woman
SYMBOL:	○+
DISCOVERER:	Adam
ATOMIC MASS:	Accepted as 55kg, but known to vary from 45kg to 225kg

PHYSICAL PROPERTIES
1. Body surface normally covered with film of powder and paint
2. Boils at absolutely nothing – freezes for no apparent reason
3. Found in various grades ranging from virgin material to common ore

CHEMICAL PROPERTIES
1. Reacts well to gold, platinum and all precious stones
2. Explodes spontaneously without reason or warning
3. The most powerful money reducing agent known to man

COMMON USE
1. Highly ornamental, especially in sports cars
2. Can greatly aid relaxation
3. Can be a very effective cleaning agent

HAZARDS
1. Turns green when placed alongside a superior specimen
2. Possession of more than one is possible but specimens must never make eye contact

There was an old guy wandering around the supermarket calling out, "Tenderflake Oh, Tenderfllllaaaakkke!" Soon a store clerk approached, "Sir, the baking goods are in aisle D." . The old gentleman replied, "Oh, I'm not looking for baking stuff. I'm calling my wife." "Your wife's name is Tenderflake?" The old man answered, "Oh no, no, no. I only call her that when we're out in public." The store clerk asked, "Well, what do you call her when you're at home?"The old man replied, "Lard Ass."

Three guys show up in front of St Peter on Christmas Eve.
"You can come in if you have something related to Christmas" says St Peter.
The first guy pulls out a lighter and flicks it "This is the candle of Christmas" he says.
"Welcome" says St Peter.
The second guy takes his keys out and jingles them "These are the bells."
"Welcome" says St Peter.
The third guy searches for something and then from his back pocket pulls out a pair of panties.
"What is that?" booms St Peter
The third man replies "They are Carol's"

A cowboy is driving down a back road in Texas... sign in front of a restaurant reads:
Happy Hour Special...Lobster Tail and Beer
"Lord almighty" he says to himself, "my three favourite things!"

What is the difference between a dog and a fox?
Four beer.

A very loud, unattractive, mean-acting woman walks into Wal-Mart with
her two kids in tow, screaming obscenities at them all the way through
the entrance.
The Wal-Mart Greeter says, "Good morning and welcome to Wal-Mart
...Nice children you've got there - are they twins?"
The ugly woman stops screaming long enough to say, "Hell no they ain't,
the oldest one, he's 9 and the younger one, she's 7. Why the hell would
you think they're twins... Do you really think they look alike?"
"No," replies the greeter, "I just couldn't believe you got laid twice.

While riding the range one day, a ventriloquist cowboy met an Indian riding along with a dog and a sheep and decided to have some fun with him.
Cowboy: "Hey, nice dog you got there. Mind if I speak to him?"
Indian: "Dog no talk."
Cowboy: "Hey dog, how's it going?"
Dog: "Doin' good."
Indian is shocked. .
Cowboy: "Is this Indian your owner?" pointing at the Indian.
Dog: "Yep"
Cowboy: "How does he treat you?"
Dog: "Real good. He lets me run free twice a day, feeds me great food, and takes me to the lake once a week to play."
Indian has a look of total disbelief.
Cowboy: "Mind if I talk to your horse?"
Indian: "Horse no talk."
Cowboy: "Hey horse, how are you?"
Horse: "Good."
Cowboy: "Is this your owner?" indicating the Indian again.

Horse: "Yep"

Cowboy: "How's he treat you?"

Horse: "Pretty good, thanks for asking. He rides me regularly, brushes me down often, and keeps me under a tree to protect me from the rain."

Indian stares in utter amazement.

Cowboy: "Mind if I talk to your sheep?"

Indian: "Sheep is liar."

Your last Car

its always a station wagon

The 3-minute management course.

Lesson 1:

A man is getting into the shower just as his wife is finishing up her shower, when the doorbell rings. The wife quickly wraps herself in a towel and runs downstairs. When she opens the door, there stands Bob the next-door neighbour. Before she says a word, Bob says, "I'll give you $800 to drop that towel."

After thinking for a moment, the woman drops her towel and stands naked in front of Bob. After a few seconds, Bob hands her $800 and leaves. The woman wraps back up in the towel and goes back upstairs.

When she gets to the bathroom, her husband asks, "Who was that?" "It was Bob the next door neighbour," she replies. "Great!" the husband says, "did he say anything about the

$800 he owes me?"

Moral of the story: If you share critical information pertaining to credit and risk with your shareholders in time, you may be in a position to prevent avoidable exposure.

Lesson 2:

A priest offered a Nun a lift. She got in and crossed her legs, forcing her gown to reveal a leg. The priest nearly had an accident. After controlling the car, he stealthily slid his hand up her leg. The nun said, "Father, remember Psalm 129?" The priest removed his hand. But, changing gears, he let his hand slide up her leg again. The nun once again said, "Father, remember Psalm 129?" The priest apologized "Sorry sister but the flesh is weak." Arriving at the convent, the nun sighed heavily and went on her way.

On his arrival at the church, the priest rushed to look up Psalm 129. It said, "Go forth and seek, further up, you will find glory."

Moral of the story: If you are not well informed in your job, you might miss a great opportunity

Lesson 3:

A sales rep, an administration clerk, and the manager are walking to lunch when they find an antique oil lamp. They rub it and a Genie comes out. The Genie says, "I'll give each of you just one wish."

"Me first! Me first!" says the admin clerk. "I want to be in the Bahamas, driving a speedboat without a care in the world." Puff! She's gone. "Me next! Me next!" says the sales rep. "I want to be in Hawaii , relaxing on the beach with my personal masseuse, an endless supply of Pina Coladas and the love of my life." Puff! He's gone. "OK, you're up," the Genie says to the manager. The manager says, "I want those two back in the office after lunch."

Moral of the story: Always let your boss have the first say.

Lesson 4:

An eagle was sitting on a tree resting, doing nothing. A small rabbit saw the eagle and asked him, "Can I also sit like you and do nothing?" The eagle answered: "Sure, why not." So, the rabbit sat on the ground

below the eagle and rested. All of a sudden, a fox appeared, jumped on the rabbit and ate it.

Moral of the story: To be sitting and doing nothing, you must be sitting very, very high up.

Lesson 5:

A turkey was chatting with a bull. "I would love to be able to get to the top of that tree," sighed the turkey, "but I haven't got the energy." "Well, why don't you nibble on some of my droppings?" replied the

bull. They're packed with nutrients." The turkey pecked at a lump of dung, and found it actually gave him enough strength to reach the lowest branch of the tree. The next day, after eating some more dung, he reached the second branch. Finally after a fourth night, the turkey was proudly perched at the top of the tree. He was promptly spotted by a farmer, who shot him out of the tree.

Moral of the story:

Bulls**t might get you to the top, but it won't keep you there.

Lesson 6:

A little bird was flying south for the winter. It was so cold the bird froze and fell to the ground into a large field. While he was lying there, a cow came by and dropped some dung on him. As the frozen bird lay there in the pile of cow dung, he began to realize how warm he was. The dung was actually thawing him out! He lay there all warm and happy, and soon began to sing for joy. A passing cat heard the bird singing and came to investigate. Following the sound, the cat discovered the bird under the pile of cow dung, and promptly dug him out and ate him.

Moral of the story:
(1) Not everyone who sh*ts on you is your enemy.
(2) Not everyone who gets you out of sh*t is your friend.
(3) And when you're in deep sh*t, it's best to keep your mouth shut!

This ends the 3-minute management course.

FAIL
That's why you always get picked last, fatty.

http://www.myconfinedspace.com/

Dear Tech Support:

Last year I upgraded from Girlfriend 7.0 to Wife 1.0 . I soon noticed that the new program began unexpected child processing that took up a lot of space and valuable resources.

In addition, Wife 1.0 installed itself into all other programs and now monitors all other system activity. Applications such as Poker Night 10.3, Football 5.0 , Hunting and Fishing 7.5 , and Golfing 3.6.

I can't seem to keep Wife 1.0 in the background while attempting to run my favorite applications. I'm thinking about going back to Girlfriend 7.0 , but the uninstall doesn't work on Wife 1.0 .

Please help!

Thanks,
Troubled User.....

REPLY:
Dear Troubled User:

This is a very common problem that men complain about.

Many people upgrade from Girlfriend 7.0 to Wife 1.0, thinking that it is just a Utilities and Entertainment program. Wife 1.0 is an OPERATING SYSTEM and is designed by its Creator to run EVERYTHING !!! It is also impossible to delete Wife 1.0 and to return to Girlfriend 7.0 . It is impossible to uninstall, or purge the program files from the system once installed.

You cannot go back to Girlfriend 7.0 because Wife 1.0 is designed to not allow this. Look in your Wife 1.0 manual under Warnings-Alimony/Child Support . I recommend that you keep Wife 1.0 and work on improving the situation. I suggest install ling the background application "Yes Dear" to alleviate software augmentation.

The best course of action is to enter the command C:\APOLOGIZE! because ultimately you will have to give the APOLOGIZE command before the system will return to normal anyway.

Wife 1.0 is a great program, but it tends to be very high maintenance. Wife 1.0 comes with several support programs, such as Clean and Sweep 3.0 , Cook It 1.5 and Do Bills 4.2 .

However, be very careful how you use these programs. Improper use will cause the system to launch the program Nag Nag 9.5 . Once this happens, the only way to improve the performance of Wife 1.0 is to purchase additional software. I recommend Flowers 2.1 and Diamonds 5.0 !

WARNING!!! DO NOT, under any circumstances, install Secretary With Short Skirt 3.3 . This application is not supported by Wife 1.0 and will cause irreversible damage to the operating system!

Best of luck,

Dell Tech Support

A Quebecois was arrested in BC for screwing an underage girl. The cop tells him " It will be OK if you have consent." The Quebecois says, "Tabernac I got dat. Let me go. I got dat cunt scent on my finger, cunt scent on my nose and cunt scent on my dick."

The bird of spring: Robin
The bird of War: Eagle
The bird of peace and love: Dove
The bird of true love: Swallow

Once again, The Washington Post has published the winning submissions to its yearly contest, in which
readers are asked to supply alternate meanings for common words.
The winners are:
1. Coffee (n.) the person upon whom one coughs.
2. Flabbergasted (adj.) appalled over how much weight you have gained.
3. Abdicate (v.) to give up all hope of ever having a flat stomach.
4. Esplanade (v.) to attempt an explanation while drunk.
5. Willy-nilly (adj.) impotent.
6. Negligent (adj.) describes a condition in which you absent-mindedly answer the door in your nightgown.
7. Lymph (v.) to walk with a lisp.
8. Gargoyle (n.) olive-flavored mouthwash.
9. Flatulence (n.) emergency vehicle that picks you up after you are run over by a steamroller.
10. Balderdash (n.) a rapidly receding hairline.
11. Testicle (n.) a humorous question on an exam.
12. Rectitude (n.) the formal, dignified bearing adopted by proctologists.
13. Pokemon (n) a Rastafarian proctologist.
14. Oyster (n.)a person who sprinkles his conversation with Yiddishisms.
15. Frisbeetarianism (n.) (back by popular demand): The belief that, when you die, your Soul flies up onto the roof and gets stuck there.
16. Circumvent (n.) an opening in the front of boxer shorts worn by Jewish men.

Make Up $60

Designer clothes $650

Boob Job $6000

Forgetting To Tuck in Your Nuts...
PRICELESS !!

I recently read that love is entirely a matter of chemistry.
That must be why my wife treats me like toxic waste.
David Bissonette

When a man steals your wife, there is no better revenge than
to let him keep her.
Sacha Guitry

After marriage, husband and wife become two sides of a coin;
they just can't face each other, but still they stay together.
Hemant Joshi

By all means marry. If you get a good wife, you'll be happy. If you get a bad one, you'll become a philosopher. Socrates

Woman inspires us to great things, and prevents us from achieving them.
Dumas

The great question... which I have not been able to answer... is, "What does a woman want?
Sigmund Freud

I had some words with my wife, and she had some paragraphs with me.
Anonymous

"Some people ask the secret of our long marriage. We take time to go to a restaurant two times a week. A little candlelight, dinner, soft music and dancing. She goes Tuesdays, I go Fridays."
Henny Youngman

"I don't worry about terrorism. I was married for two years."
Sam Kinison

"There's a way of transferring funds that is even faster than electronic banking. It's called marriage."
James Holt McGavran

"I've had bad luck with both my wives. The first one left me, and the second one didn't."
Patrick Murray

Two secrets to keep your marriage brimming
1. Whenever you're wrong, admit it,
2. Whenever you're right, shut up.
Nash

———

The most effective way to remember your wife's birthday is to forget it once...
Anonymous

You know what I did before I married? Anything I wanted to.
Henny Youngman

My wife and I were happy for twenty years. Then we met.
Rodney Dangerfield

A good wife always forgives her husband when she's wrong.
Milton Berle

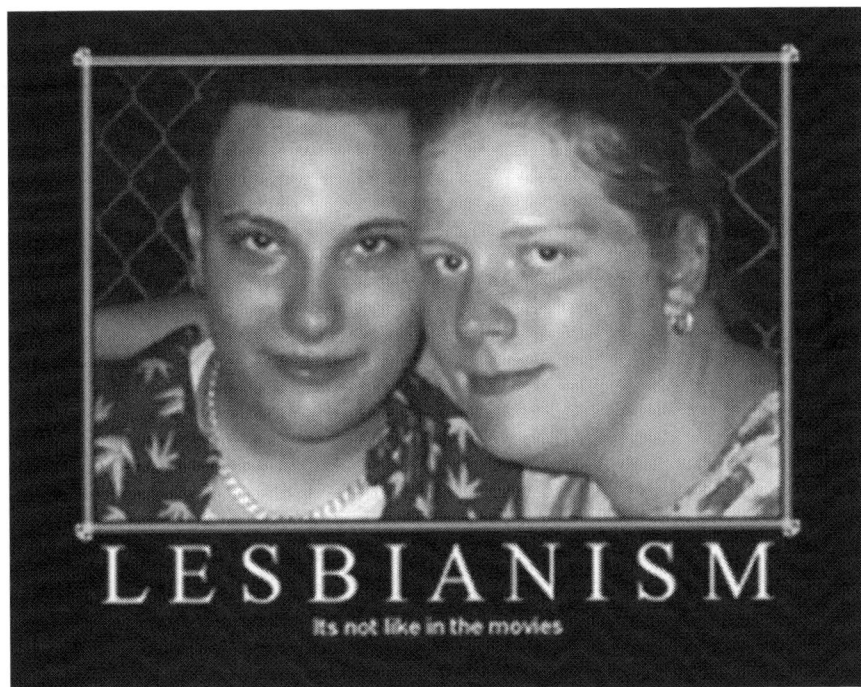

LESBIANISM
Its not like in the movies

Marriage is the only war where one sleeps with the enemy.
Anonymous

A man inserted an 'ad' in the classifieds: "Wife wanted". Next day he received a hundred letters. They all said the same thing: "You can have mine."

First Guy (proudly): "My wife's an angel!"
Second Guy: "You're lucky, mine's still alive."

She is in the kitchen preparing to boil eggs for breakfast. He walks in. She turns and says, "You've got to make love to me this very moment." His eyes light up and he thinks, This is my lucky day." Not wanting to lose the moment, he embraces her and then gives it his all on the kitchen table. Afterwards she says, "Thanks," and returns to the stove. More than a little puzzled, he asks, "What was that all about?"
She explains, "The egg timer's broken."

In Pharmacology, all drugs have two names: a trade name and a generic name. For example, the trade name Tylenol is acetaminophen. Aleve is known as naproxen, Amoxil is amoxicillin. Advil is ibuprophen. The   FDA has been looking for a generic name for Viagra. After consideration by a team of experts, it recently announced it has settled on the generic name of mycoxafloppin. Also considered were mycoxafailin, mydixadrupin, mydixarizin, mydixadud, dixafix, and of course ibepokin. Pfizer Corp. is making an announcement today that Viagra will soon be available in liquid form and will be marketed by Pepsi Cola as a power beverage suitable for use as a mixer. Pepsi's proposed ad campaign claims it will now be possible for a man to literally pour himself a stiff one.

Obviously, we can no longer call this a soft drink. This additive gives new meaning to the names of Cocktails and Highballs. Pepsi will market the new formula by the name, Mount & Do.

The long term implications of drugs and medical procedures must be fully considered: Over the past five years, Americans have spent more money on breast implants and Viagra than was spent on Alzheimer's research. It is believed that by the year 2030, there will be a large number of people wandering around with perky breasts and erections who can't remember what to do with them.

A guy is driving around Tennessee and he sees a sign in front of a house. "Talking Dog for Sale." He rings the bell and the owner tells him the dog is in the backyard. The guy goes into the backyard and sees a Labrador retriever sitting there. "You talk?" he asks. "Yes, I do," the Lab replies. "So, what's your story?" The Lab looks up and says, "Well, I discovered that I could talk when I was pretty young.

I wanted to help the government, so I told the CIA about my gift, and in no time at all they had me jetting from country to country, sitting in rooms with spies and world leaders, because no one figured a dog would be eavesdropping. I was one of their most valuable spies for eight years running. But the jetting around really tired me out, and I knew I wasn't getting any younger so I decided to settle down. I signed up for a job at the airport to do some undercover security wandering near suspicious characters and listening in. I uncovered some incredible dealings and was awarded a batch of medals. I got married, had a mess of puppies, and now I'm just retired." The guy is amazed. He goes back in and asks the owner what he wants for the dog. "Ten dollars," the guy says. "Ten dollars!!? Is that all? This dog is amazing. Why on earth are you selling him so cheap?" "Because he's a liar. He never did any of that shit."

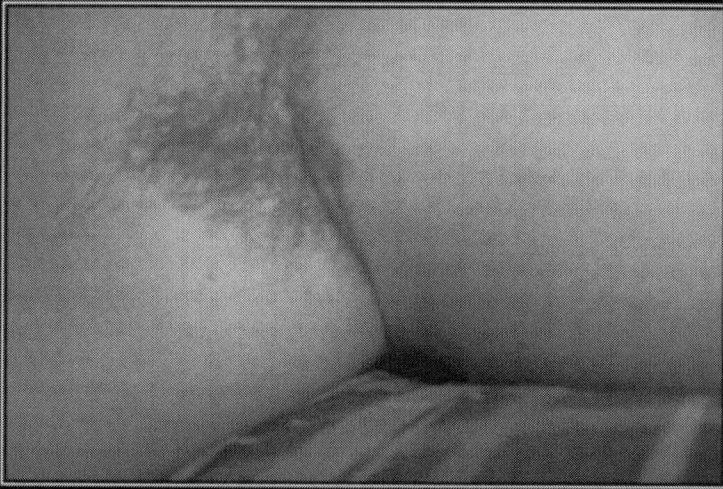

RELAX
it's just my armpit

MARY HAD A LITTLE LAMB
Her father shot it dead.
Now it goes to school with her,
Between two hunks of bread.
                ****

JACK AND JILL Went up the hill
To have a little fun.
Stupid Jill forgot the pill
And now they have a son.
                ****

SIMPLE SIMON met a Pie man going to the fair.
Said Simple Simon to the Pie man,
What have you got there?"
Said the Pie man unto Simon,
Pies, you Dumb Ass"
                ****

HUMPTY DUMPTY sat on a wall,
Humpty Dumpty had a great fall.
All the kings' horses,
And all the kings' men.
Had scrambled eggs,
For breakfast again.
                ****

HEY DIDDLE, DIDDLE the cat took a piddle,
All over the bedside clock.
The little dog laughed to see such fun.
Then died of electric shock.
                ****

GEORGIE PORGY Pudding and Pie,
Kissed the girls and made them cry.
And when the boys came out to play,
He kissed them too 'cause he was gay.
                ****

Mary had a little pig,
 She kept it fat and plastered;
And when the price of pork went up,
She shot the little bastard.

There was a little girl who had a little curl
Right in the middle of her forehead.
When she was good, she was very, very good.
But when she was bad........
She got a fur coat, jewels, a waterfront condo, and a sports car.

Definitions
Arbitrator \ar'-bi-tray-ter\:A cook that leaves Arby's to work at McDonalds
Seamstress \seem'-stres\: describes 250 pounds in a size 6
Subdued \sub-dood'\: like, a guy, like works on one of those, like, submarines, man

ELEPHANTS

Larger than the moon

Canadian Temperature Guide

50° Fahrenheit (10° C)
Californians shiver uncontrollably,
Canadians plant gardens.

35° Fahrenheit (1.6° C)
Italian cars won't start,
Canadians drive with the windows down.

32° Fahrenheit (0° C)
American water freezes,
Canadian water gets thicker.

0° Fahrenheit (-17.9° C)
New York City landlords finally turn on the heat,
Canadians have the last barbecue of the season.

-60° Fahrenheit (-51° C)
Mt. St. Helens freezes,
Canadians Girl Guides sell cookies door to door.

-100° Fahrenheit (-73° C)
Santa Claus abandons the North Pole,
Ottawa canal opens for skating.

-173° Fahrenheit (-114° C)
Ethyl alcohol freezes,
Canadians get frustrated when they can't thaw the keg.

-460° Fahrenheit (-273° C)
Absolute zero; all atomic motion stops,
Canadians start saying "cold eh?"

-500° Fahrenheit (-295° C)
Hell freezes over,
Vancouver wins Stanley Cup.

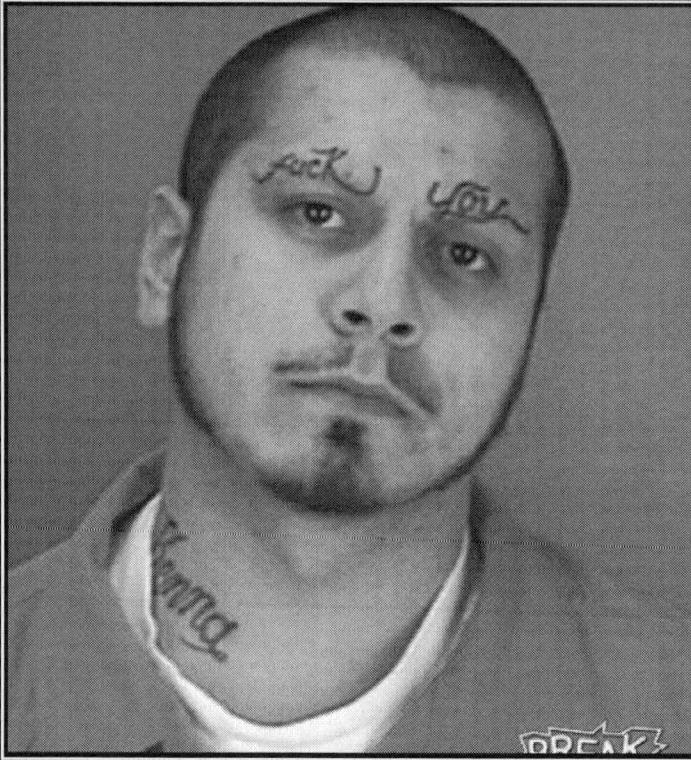

SELF EXPRESSION
Feel Free To Let People Know How You Really Feel.

AMAZINGLY SIMPLE HOME REMEDIES

1. A mouse trap, placed on top of your alarm clock, will prevent you from rolling over and going back to sleep after you hit the snooze button.

2. If you have a bad cough, take a large dose of laxatives, then you will be afraid to cough.

3. Clumsy? Avoid cutting yourself while slicing vegetables by getting someone else to hold them while
you chop away.

4. Avoid arguments with the Mrs. about lifting the toilet seat by simply using the sink.

5. For high blood pressure sufferers: simply cut yourself and bleed for a few minutes, thus reducing
the pressure in your veins. Remember to use a timer.

6. Have a bad toothache? Smash your thumb with a hammer and you will forget about the toothache.

Sometimes, we just need to remember what the rules of life really are.

You only need two tools: WD-40 and Duct Tape.
If it doesn't move and should, use the WD-40.
If it shouldn't move and does, use the duct tape.

Remember:
Everyone seems normal until you get to know them. * Never pass up an opportunity to go to the bathroom.
* If you woke up breathing, congratulations! You get another chance.

And finally, be really nice to your family and friends; you never know when you might need them to
empty your bedpan.

Q: Why do airports have runways?
A: So the handicapped can fly

A man appeared before St. Peter at the Pearly Gates. "Have you ever done anything of particular merit?" St. Peter asked. "Well, I can think of one thing," the man offered. "Once, on a trip to the Black Hills out in South Dakota , I came upon a gang of bikers, who were threatening a young woman. I directed them to leave her alone, but they wouldn't listen. So, I approached the largest and most heavily tattooed biker and smacked him in his face, kicked his bike over, ripped out his nose ring, and threw it on the ground. I yelled, "Now, back off!! Or I'll kick the "sh*t" out of all of you!" St. Peter was impressed, "When did this happen?"
"Just a couple of minutes ago."

Sex is like snooker, if your shooting for the pink, and blocked by the red. Go for the brown.

A woman runs into a Police station" she yells I've been raped by a Helicopter Pilot.
The sergeant says how do you know he's a Pilot? Well she says, He had a Big Watch and a Little dick and couldn't stop talking about himself!.

The nipples of Susan Sarong
When erect were big, fat and long
My plans went askew
When I found out that Sue
Expected no less from my schlong

Do infants enjoy infancy as much as adults enjoy adultery?
 If love is blind, why is lingerie so popular?
Why is the man who invests all your money called a broker?
There is no egg in the eggplant, no ham in the hamburger and neither pine nor apple in the pineapple. English muffins were not invented in England, French fries were not invented in France.

Taken from the Guardian, an actual letter sent by the Inland Revenue:

Dear Mr. Addison,

I am writing to you to express our thanks for your more than prompt reply to our latest communication, and also to answer some of the points you raise. I will address them, as ever, in order.

Firstly, I must take issue with your description of our last as a "begging letter". It might perhaps more properly be referred to as a "tax demand".
This is how we at the Inland Revenue have always, for reasons of accuracy, traditionally referred to such documents.

Secondly, your frustration at our adding to the "endless stream of crapulent whining and panhandling vomited daily through the letterbox on to the doormat" has been noted. However, whilst I have naturally not seen the other letters to which you refer I would cautiously suggest that their being from "pauper councils, Lombardy pirate banking houses and pissant gas-mongers" might indicate that your decision to "file them next to the toilet in case of emergencies" is at best a little ill-advised. In common with my own organization, it is unlikely that the senders of these letters do see you as a "lackwit bumpkin" or, come to that, a "sodding charity". More likely they see you as a citizen of Great Britain, with a responsibility to contribute to the upkeep of the nation as a whole.

Which brings me to my next point. Whilst there may be some spirit of truth in your assertion that the taxes you pay "go to shore up the canker-blighted, toppling folly that is the Public Services", a moment's rudimentary calculation ought to disabuse you of the notion that the government in any way expects you to "stump up for the whole damned party" yourself. The estimates you provide for the Chancellor's disbursement of the funds levied by taxation, whilst colourful, are, in fairness, a little off the mark. Less than you seem to imagine is spent on "junkets for Bunterish lickspittles" and "dancing whores" whilst far more than you have accounted for is allocated to, for example, "that box-ticking façade of a university system."

A couple of technical points arising from direct queries:
1. The reason we don't simply write "Muggins" on the envelope has to do with the vagaries of the postal system;
2. You can rest assured that "sucking the very marrows of those with nothing else to give" has never been considered as a practice because even if the Personal Allowance didn't render it irrelevant, the sheer medical logistics involved would make it financially unviable.

I trust this has helped. In the meantime, whilst I would not in any way wish to influence your decision one way or the other, I ought to point out that even if you did choose to "give the whole foul jamboree up and go and live in India" you would still owe us the money. Please send it to us by Friday.

Yours sincerely,

H J Lee Customer Relations

1. Do not walk behind me, for I may not lead. Do not walk ahead of me, or I may not follow. Do not walk beside me either. Just pretty much leave me alone.

2 The journey of a thousand miles begins with a broken fan belt and leaky tire.

3. It's always darkest before dawn. So if you're going to steal your neighbour's newspaper, that's the time to do it.

TEAM PLAYER

BECAUSE SOMEONE HAS TO TAKE THE FAT GIRL HOME.

4. Don't be irreplaceable. If you can't be replaced, you can't be promoted.

5. Always remember that you're unique. Just like everyone else.

6. Never test the depth of the water with both feet.

7. If you think nobody cares if you're alive, try missing a couple of car payments.

8. Before you criticize someone, you should walk a mile in their shoes. That way, when you criticize them, you're a mile away and you have their shoes.

9. If at first you don't succeed, skydiving is not for you.

10. Give a man a fish and he will eat for a day. Teach him how

to fish, and he will sit in a boat and drink beer all day.

11. If you lend someone $20 and never see that person again, it was probably worth it.

12. If you tell the truth, you don't have to remember anything.

13. Some days you're the bug; some days you're the windshield.

14. Everyone seems normal until you get to know them.

15. The quickest way to double your money is to fold it in half and put it back in your pocket.

16. A closed mouth gathers no foot.

17. Duct tape is like 'The Force'. It has a light side and a dark side, and it holds the universe together.

18. There are two theories to arguing with women. Neither one works.

19. Generally speaking, you aren't learning much when your lips are moving.

20. Experience is something you don't get until just after you need it.

21. Never miss a good chance to shut up

Why Helicopters are Better than Women

1. A helicopter will kill you quickly . . . a woman takes her time.

2. Helicopters can be turned on by a flick of a switch.

3. A helicopter does not get mad if you 'touch and go.'

4. A helicopter does not object to a preflight inspection.

5. Helicopters come with manuals.

6. Helicopters have strict weight and balance limits.

7. You can fly a helicopter any time of the month.

8. Helicopters don't come with in-laws.

9. Helicopters don't whine unless something is really wrong.

10. Helicopters don't care about how many other helicopters you have flown.

11. When flying, you and your helicopter both arrive at the same time.

12. Helicopters don't mind if you look at other helicopters, or if you buy helicopter magazines.

13. It's OK to use tie-downs on your helicopter.

Man goes into a cocktail lounge and approaches Maxine sitting by herself

Man: "May I buy you a cocktail?"
Maxine: "No thank you, alcohol is bad for my legs."

Man: "Sorry to hear that. Do they swell?"
Maxine: "No, they spread."

A mother took her five-year-old son with her to the bank on a busy lunchtime. They got behind a very fat woman wearing a business suit complete with pager. As they waited patiently, the little boy said loudly, "Gee, she's fat!" The mother bent down and whispered in the little boys ear to be quiet. A couple of minutes passed by and the little boy spread his hands as far as they would go and announced; "I'll bet her butt is this wide!" The fat woman turns around and glares at the little boy. The mother gave him a good telling off, and told him to be quiet. After a brief lull, the large woman reached the front of the line. Just then her pager begin to emit a beep, beep, beep. The little boy yells out, "Run for your f---'n life, she's backing up!!"

A large woman, wearing a sleeveless sundress, walked into a bar in Dublin. She raised her right arm, revealing a huge, hairy armpit as she pointed to all the people sitting at the bar and asked, "What man here

Will buy a lady a drink?" The bar went silent as the patrons tried to ignore her. But down at the end of the bar, an owly-eyed drunk slammed his hand down on the counter and bellowed, "Give the ballerina a drink!" The bartender poured the drink and the woman chugged it down. She turned to the patrons and again pointed around at all of them, revealing the same hairy armpit, and asked, "What man here will buy a lady a drink?" Once again, the same little drunk slapped his money down on the bar and said, "Give the ballerina another drink!" The bartender approached the little drunk and said, "Tell me, Paddy,
it's your business if you want to buy the lady a drink, but why do you keep calling her the ballerina?"
The drunk replied, "Any woman who can lift her leg that high has got to be a ballerina!"

Sign over a Gynecologist's Office: "Dr. Jones, at your cervix."
In a Podiatrist's office: "Time wounds all heels."
On a Septic Tank Truck in Oregon: Yesterday's Meals on Wheels
On another Septic Tank Truck: "We're #1 in the #2 business"
At a Proctologist's door: "To expedite your visit please back in.
On a Plumber's truck: "We repair what your husband fixed."
On another Plumber's truck: "Don't sleep with a drip. Call your plumber."
On a Church's Billboard: "7 days without God makes one weak."
At a Tire Shop in Milwaukee "Invite us to your next blowout."
On a Plastic Surgeon's Office door: "Hello. Can we pick your nose?
At a Towing company: "We don't charge an arm and a leg. We want tows.

On an Electrician's truck: "Let us remove your shorts."
In a Nonsmoking Area: "If we see smoke, we will assume you are on fire and take appropriate action."
On a Maternity Room door: "Push. Push. Push."
At an Optometrist's Office: "If you don't see what you're looking for, you've come to the right place."
On a Taxidermist's window: "We really know our stuff."
On a Fence: "Salesmen welcome! Dog food is expensive!"
At a Car Dealership: "The best way to get back on your feet - miss a car payment."
Outside a Muffler Shop: "No appointment necessary. We hear you coming."
In a Veterinarian's waiting room: "Be back in 5 minutes. Sit! Stay!"
At the Electric Company: "We would be delighted if you send in your payment. However, if you don't, you will be."
In a Restaurant window: "Don't stand there and be hungry, Come on in and get fed up."
In the front yard of a Funeral Home: "Drive carefully. We'll wait."
At a Propane Filling Station: "Thank heaven for little grills."
Sign at a Chicago Radiator Shop: "Best place in town to take a leak."

The local drunk walks into a bar and orders a soda. The bar tender asks him why not his regular drink.
"I have been drinking too much" says the regular, "Last night, I blew chunks."
"That is OK," says the bar tender "Everybody does that once in a while."
"No you don't understand – Chunks is my dog."

PROCRASTINATION
is like masturbation...it's good in the beginning, but in the end, you realize
you've just fucked yourself

Why sentence structure is so important. The boss was facing cutbacks and had to let somebody go. He narrowed it down to one of two people, Debra or Jack. It was an impossible decision because they were both super workers. Rather than flip a coin, he decided he would dismiss the first one who used the water cooler the next morning. Debra came in the next morning with a horrible hangover after partying all night. She went to the cooler to take an aspirin. The boss approached her and said: 'Debra, I've never done this before > but I have to lay you or Jack off.' 'Could you jack off?' she says. 'I feel like shit.'

Subject: THE INDIAN AND THE GAY GUY At the end of a tiny deserted bar sits a huge Indian. He's having a few beers when a short, well dressed, and obviously gay man walks in and sits down beside him. After three or four beers the gay fellow finally picks up the courage to say something to the big Indian. Leaning over towards him, he whispers, "Do you want a blow job?" At this the massive Indian leaps up, with fire in his eyes, and smacks > the man in the face knocking him swiftly off his stool. He proceeds to beat him all the way out of the bar before leaving him bruised and battered in the parking lot and returning to his seat. Amazed, the bartender quickly brings over another beer to the big > Indian. "I've never seen you react like that," he says. "Just what did he say to you?". "I don't know," the big Indian replied. "Something about a job."

One day my mother was out and my dad was in charge of me. I was maybe 2 1/2 years old and had just recovered from an accident. Someone had given me a little 'tea set' as a get-well gift and it was one of my favorite toys. Daddy was in the living room engrossed in the evening news when I brought Daddy a little cup of 'tea', which was just water. After several cups of tea and lots of praise for such yummy tea, my Mom came home. My Dad made her wait in the living room to watch me bring him a cup of tea, because it was 'just the cutest thing!' My Mom waited, and sure enough, here I come down the hall with a cup of tea for Daddy and she watches him drink it up. Then she says, (as only a mother would know... :) 'Did it ever occur to you that the only place she can reach to get water is the toilet?'

PREGNANCY
DON'T FORGET TO PULL OUT

Ten Reasons Men Prefer Guns Over Women #10. You can trade an old .44 for a new .22. #9. You can keep one gun at home and have another for when you're on the road. #8. If you admire a friend's gun and tell him so, he will probably let you try it out a few times. #7. Your primary gun doesn't mind if you keep another gun for a backup. #6. Your gun will stay with you even if you run out of ammo. #5. A gun doesn't take up a lot of closet space. #4. Guns function normally every day of the month. #3. A gun doesn't ask, "Do these new grips make me look fat?" #2. A gun doesn't mind if you go to sleep after you use it. #1. YOU CAN BUY A SILENCER FOR A GUN

Lawyers should never ask a Mississippi grandma a question if they aren't prepared for the answer. In a trial, a Southern small-town prosecuting attorney called his first witness, a grandmotherly, elderly woman to the stand. He approached her and asked, "Mrs. Jones, do you know me?" She responded, "Why, yes, I do know you, Mr. Williams. I've known you since you were a young boy, and frankly, you've been a big disappointment to me. You lie, you cheat on your wife, and you manipulate people and talk about them behind their backs. You think you're a big shot when you haven't the brains to realize you never will amount to anything more than a two-bit paper pusher. Yes, I know you." The lawyer was stunned! Not knowing what else to do, he pointed across the room and asked, "Mrs. Jones, do you know the defense attorney?" She again replied, "Why, yes, I do. I've known Mr. Bradley since he was a youngster, too. He's lazy, bigoted, and he has a drinking problem. He can't build a normal relationship with anyone and his law practice is one of the worst in the entire state. Not to mention he cheated on his wife with three different women. One of them was your wife. Yes, I know him." The defense attorney almost died. The judge asked both counselors to approach the bench and, in a very quiet voice, said, "If either of you idiots asks her if she knows me, I'll send you to the electric chair."

First-year students at Texas A&M's Vet school were receiving their first anatomy class, with a real dead cow. They all gathered around the surgery table with the body covered with a white sheet. The professor started the class by telling them, 'In Veterinary Medicine it is necessary to have two important qualities as a doctor.

The first is that you not be disgusted by anything involving the animal body. For an example, the Professor pulled back the sheet, stuck his finger in the butt of the dead cow, withdrew it and stuck it in his mouth. 'Go ahead and do the same thing,' he told his students. The students freaked out, hesitated for several minutes. But eventually took turns sticking a finger in the anal opening of the dead cow and sucking on it.

When everyone finished, the Professor looked at them and said, 'The second most important quality is observation. I stuck in my middle finger and sucked on my index finger. Now learn to pay attention.' Life's tough, it's even tougher if you're stupid.'

There is a new study just released by the American Psychiatric Association about women and how they feel about their asses. The results are pretty interesting: 5% of women surveyed feel their ass is too big. 10% of women surveyed feel their ass is too small. The remaining 85% say they don't care; they love him; he's a good man, and they would have married him anyway.

A female CNN journalist heard about a very old Jewish man who had been going to the Western Wall to pray, twice a day, every day, for a long, long time. So she went to check it out. She went to the Western Wall and there he was, walking slowly up to the holy site. She watched him pray and after about 45 minutes, when he turned to leave, using a cane and moving very slowly, she approached him for an interview.

"Pardon me, sir, I'm Rebecca Smith from CNN. What's your name?" Morris Fishbien," he replied. "Sir, how long have you been coming to the Western Wall and praying?" "For about 60 years.""60 years! That's amazing! What do you pray for?" "I pray for peace between the Christians, Jews and the Muslims." "I pray for all the wars and all the hatred to stop." "I pray for all our children to grow up safely as responsible adults, and to love their fellow man." "How do you feel after doing this for 60 years?""Like I'm talking to a fuckin' wall."

JIU JITSU
It's only gay if you make eye contact.

InsideFighting.com

The next time someone asks you a dumb question wouldn't you like to respond like this?.....

Yesterday I was buying a large bag of Purina dog chow for my kid's dogs (Kodiak, Jersey and Leo) at Wal-Mart and was about to check out. A woman behind me asked if I had a dog. What did she think I had. an elephant? So since I'm retired, with little to do, on impulse, I told her that no, I didn't have a dog, and that I was starting the Purina Diet again. Although I probably shouldn't, because I'd ended up in the hospital last time, but that I'd lost 50 pounds before I awakened in an intensive care ward with tubes coming out of most of my orifices and IVs in both arms. I told her that it was essentially a perfect diet. The way that it works is to load your pants pockets with Purina nuggets and simply eat one or two every time you feel hungry and that the food is nutritionally complete so I was going to try it again.

 (I have to mention here that practically everyone in the line was by now enthralled with my story.)

Horrified, she asked if I ended up in intensive care because the dog food poisoned me. I told her no, I stepped off a curb to sniff an Irish Setter's ass and a car hit us both.

I thought the guy behind her was going to have a heart attack, he was laughing so hard!

WAL-MART won't let me shop there anymore!!!

Sven & Olaf were fishing one day when Sven pulled out a cigar. Finding he had no matches, he asked Olaf for a light. 'Ya, shure, I tink I haff a lighter', he replied. Then reaching into his tackle box, he pulled out a Bic lighter 10 inches long. 'Yiminy Cricket!' exclaimed Sven, taking the huge Bic Lighter in his hands. Vere dit yew git dat monster??'

'Vell', replied Olaf, 'I got it from my Genie'

'You haff a Genie?' Sven asked.

'Ya, shure, it's right here in my tackle box, says Olaf.

'Could I see him?' asked Sven.

Olaf opens his tackle box & sure enough, out pops the Genie. Addressing the Genie, Sven says, 'Hey dere, I'm a good friend of your master. Vill you grant me vun vish?'

'Yes, I will', says the Genie.

So Sven asks the Genie for a million bucks.

The Genie disappears back into the tackle box leaving Sven sitting there, waiting for his million bucks. Shortly, the sky darkens and is filled with the sound of a million ducks... flying overhead.

Over the roar of the million ducks Sven yells at Olaf, 'Yumpin'Yimminy! I asked for a million bucks, not a million ducks!'

Olaf answers, 'Ya, I forgot to tell yew dat da Genie is hart of hearing. Do yew really tink I asked for a 10-inch Bic?'

MOOSEKNUCKLE
Because camel toe has an ugly sister.

The inventor of the Harley-Davidson motorcycle, Arthur Davidson, died and went to heaven. At the pearly gates, St. Peter told Arthur, "Since you've been such good man and your motorcycles have changed the world, your reward is, you can hang out with anyone you want in Heaven." Arthur thought about this for a minute and then said, "I want to hang out with God." St. Peter took Arthur to the Throne Room and introduced him to God. God recognized Arthur and commented, "Okay, so you were the one who invented the Harley Davidson motorcycle?" Arthur said, "Yep, that's me.' God said, "Well, what's the big deal in inventing something that's pretty unstable, makes noise and pollution and can't run without a road?" Arthur was apparently embarrassed, but finally he said, "Excuse me, but aren't you the inventor of woman?" God said, "Yes." "Well," said Arthur, "professional to professional, you have some major design flaws in your invention:
1. There's too much inconsistency in the front-end protrusions;
2. It chatters constantly at high speeds;
3. Most of the rear ends are too soft and wobble too much;
4. The intake is placed way too close to the exhaust;
5.. And the maintenance costs are enormous!"
"Hmmmmm, you have some good points there," replied God, "hold on." God went to His Celestial super computer, typed in some key words and waited for the results. The computer printed out a slip of paper and God read it. "Well, it may be true that my invention is flawed," God said to Arthur,"but according to these statistics, more men are riding my invention than yours."

Why is Ukrainian Christmas two weeks late? Because they can't find 3 wise men and a virgin.

What do you call a monkey in a mine field?
A Baboom.

A railroader goes to the supermarket in Waldheim and notices an attractive woman waving at him. She says hello. He's rather taken back because he can't place where he knows her from. So he says, 'Do you know me?' To which she replies, 'I think you're the father of one of my kids.' Now his mind travels back to the only time he has ever been unfaithful to his wife and says, 'My God, are you the stripper from my bachelor
party in Martensville that I made love to on the pool table with all my buddies watching while your partner whipped my butt with wet celery? She looks into his eyes and says calmly, ' No, I'm your son's teacher.'

The teacher was having a bad day and asked, "Just how stupid are you kids? Any stupid kids here please stand up." Uncomfortable silence is followed by Joe standing up. "So you think you are stupid?" she asked "No" he replied" I just didn't want you standing up all by yourself."

RETARDS

WE ALL KNOW ONE

What is long, brown and sticky?
A stick.

An idiot is walking along the river and sees another idiot on the opposite bank. He calls out "How do I get to the other side?" The other idiot replies "You already are on the other side."

An old BC couple drives into an Alberta full serve gas station. The attendant says, "I see you are from BC." The old woman who is somewhat deaf yells, "What did he say?" The husband replies, "He says we are from BC." The attendant says "I visited BC once." The old woman says, "What did he say?" The husband replies "He said he visited BC once." The attendant says, "I had the lousiest sex of my life there." The old woman says, "What did he say?" The husband replies, "He says he knows you."

How do you make a woman sound like a dolphin? Spoon her, rub your woody against her asshole and she will say "Uh uh. Uh uh.

Little Sally came home from school and with a smile on her face and told her mother,
"Frankie Brown showed me his weenie today!" Before the mother could raise a concern, Sally went on to say, "It reminded me of a peanut." Relaxing with a hidden smile, Sally's Mum asked, "Really small was it?"
Sally replied, "No... salty!"

A father watched his young daughter playing in the garden. He smiled as he reflected on how sweet and pure his little girl was. Tears formed in his eyes as he thought about her seeing the wonders. Suddenly she just stopped and stared at the ground. He went over to her to see what work of God had captured her attention. He noticed she was looking at two spiders mating. "Daddy, what are those two spiders doing?" she asked. "They're mating," her father replied. "What do you call the spider on top?" she asked. "That's a Daddy Longlegs," her father answered. "So, the other one is a Mommy Longlegs?" the little girl asked. As his heart soared with the joy of such a cute and innocent question he replied "No dear. Both of them are Daddy Longlegs." The little girl, looking a little puzzled, thought for a moment, then took her foot and stomped them flat, saying "Well, we're not having any of that brokeback mountain shit in our garden." Brings a tear to your eye...doesn't it.

  Celibacy can be a choice in life, or a condition imposed by circumstances. While attending a Marriage Encounter Weekend, Walter and his wife Ann, listened to the instructor declare" It is essential that husbands and wives know the things that Are important to each other. He addressed the men, "Can you name and describe your wife's favorite flower?" Walter leaned over, touched Ann's arm gently and whispered, "Robin Hood-All-Purpose, isn't it? "And thus began Walter's life of celibacy.

Two animal rights defenders were protesting the cruelty of sending pigs to a slaughterhouse in Bonn, Germany. Suddenly, all two thousand pigs broke loose and escaped through a broken fence, stampeding madly. The two helpless protesters were trampled to death.

188

Best 'Out of Office' Automatic e-mail Replies: 1. I am currently out of the office at a job interview and will reply to you if I fail to get the position. Please be prepared for my mood. 2. You are receiving this automatic notification because I am out of the office. If I was in, chances are you wouldn't have received anything at all. 3. Sorry to have missed you, but I'm at the doctor's having my brain and heart removed so I can be promoted to our management team. 4. I will be unable to delete all the emails you send me until I return from vacation. Please be patient, and your mail will be deleted in the order it was received. 5. Thank you for your email. Your credit card has been charged $5.99 for the first 10 words and $1.99 for each additional word in your message. 6. The email server is unable to verify your server connection.
Your message has not been delivered. Please restart your computer and try sending again. (The beauty of this is that when you return, you can see who did this over and over and over....) 7. Thank you for your message, which has been added to a queuing system. You are currently in 352nd place, and can expect to receive a reply in approximately 19 weeks. 8. Hi, I'm thinking about what you've just sent me. Please wait by your PC for my response. 9. I've run away to join a different circus. 10. I will be out of the office for the next two weeks for medical reasons. When I return, please refer to me as 'Susan' instead of Steve.

2008 Tax Code

 The only thing that the Canadian government has not taxed yet is the male penis. This is due to the fact that 69% of the time it is hanging around unemployed,

10% of the time it is hard up,

20% of the time it is pissed off

and 1% of the time it is in the hole.

On top of that, it has two dependents and they are both nuts! However, effective January 1st, 2008, the penis will now be taxed according to size: the brackets are as follows: 10"- 12" Luxury Tax $300.00 8" - 10" Pole Tax; $250.00 5" - 8" Privilege Tax $150.00 3" - 5" Nuisance Tax $30.00 Males exceeding 12" must file capital gains. Anyone under 3" is eligible for a tax refund.

PLEASE DO NOT ASK FOR AN EXTENSION!

AMAZINGLY SIMPLE HOME REMEDIES 1. If you are choking on an ice cube simply pour a cup of boiling water down your throat. Presto! The blockage will instantly remove itself. 2. Avoid cutting yourself slicing vegetables by getting someone else to hold while you chop. 3. Avoid arguments with the Mrs. about lifting the toilet seat by using the shower. 4. For high blood pressure sufferers: simply cut yourself and bleed for a few minutes, thus reducing the pressure in your veins. Remember to use a timer. 5. A mouse trap, placed on top of your alarm clock, will prevent you from rolling over and going back to sleep after you hit the snooze button. 6. If you have a bad cough, take a large dose of laxatives, then you will be afraid to cough. 7. You only need two tools in life - WD-40 and Duct Tape. If it doesn't move and should, use the WD-40. If it shouldn't move and does, use the duct tape. 8. Remember: Everyone seems normal until you get to know them. Daily Thought: SOME PEOPLE ARE LIKE SLINKYS. NOT REALLY GOOD FOR ANYTHING BUT THEY BRING A SMILE TO YOUR FACE WHEN PUSHED DOWN THE STAIRS.

PLAY DUMB

If she looks TOO young..just assume she is 18

A man gets up one morning to find his wife in the kitchen cooking. He looks to see what she's cooking, and sees one of his socks in frying pan. 'What are you doing?' he asks. 'I'm doing what you asked me to do last night when you came to bed very drunk,' she replied. Completely puzzled, the man walks away thinking to himself, 'I don't remember asking her to cook my sock......'

A guy applies for work and seems very qualified – "where did you get your education?" Yale is the answer. Good you are hired. What is your name? Jens Jorgenson.]

A woman was very distraught at the fact that she had not had a date or any sex in quite some time. She was afraid she might have something wrong with her, so she decided to seek the medical expertise of a sex therapist. Her doctor recommended that she see the well known Chinese sex therapist Dr. Chang.

So she went to see him. Upon entering the examination room Dr. Chang said "OK take off all your crose". The woman did as she was told. "Now get down and craw reery, reery fass to odderside of room". Again the woman did as she was instructed. Dr. Chang then said, "OK, now craw reery, reery fass back to me". So she did. Dr.Chang shook his head slowly and said "Your probrem vewy bad. You haf Ed Zachary disease. Worse case I ever see. Dat why you not haf sex or dates". Worried the woman asked anxiously "Oh my God Dr.Chang what is Ed Zachary Disease?" Dr. Chang sighed deeply and replied "Ed Zachary Disease is when your face look Ed Zachary like your ass".

FLEXIBILITY
It is almost never, ever over-rated.

A man and a woman who had never met before but were both married to other people found them selves assigned to the same sleeping compartment on a trans-continental train. Though initially embarrassed and uneasy over sharing a room, they were both very tired and fell asleep quickly -- he in the upper bunk and she in the lower.

At 1 a.m., the man leaned down and gently woke the woman saying, "Ma'am, I'm sorry to bother you, but would you be willing to reach into the closet and get me a second blanket? I'm awfully cold."

"I have a better idea," she replied. "Just for tonight, let's pretend that we're married."

"Wow! That's a great idea!" he exclaimed.

"Good," she replied. "Get your own fuckin' blanket."

After a moment of silence, he farted.

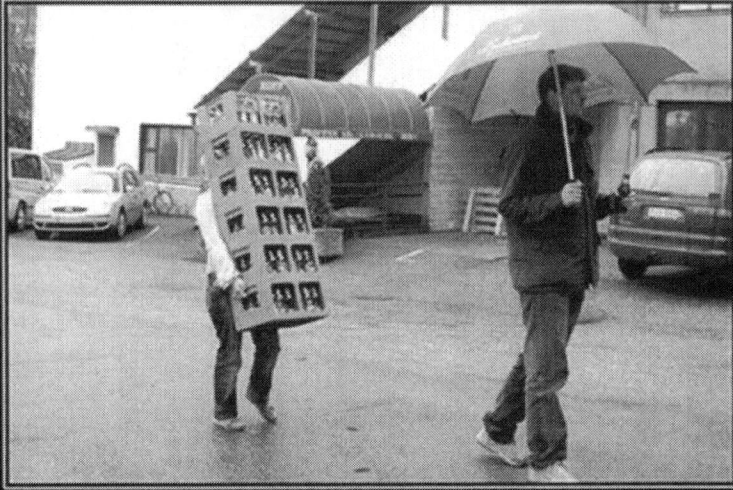

A WIFE

Because beer is heavy

An Irishman, an Englishman and a Scot were sitting in a bar. The view was fantastic, the beer excellent, and the food exceptional.

"Y'ken," said the Scotsman, "I still prefer the pubs back hame. Why, in Glasgow there's a wee bar called McTavish's.

Now, the landlord there goes out of his way for the locals so much that when you buy 4 drinks, he will buy the 5th drink for you."

"Well," said the Englishman, "at my local, The Red Lion, the barman there will buy you your 3rd drink after you buy the first two."

"Ahhh, that's nuttin," said the Irishman. "Back home in Dublin there's O'Driscoll's Bar.

Now, the moment you set foot in the place they'll buy you a drink, then another, all the drinks you like.

Then, when you've had enough drinks, they'll take you upstairs and see that you get laid. All on the house."

194

"Well," said the Englishman, "did this actually happen to you?"

"Not me myself, personally, no," said the Irishman, "but it did happen to me sister."

JAILBAIT
You keep getting older and they stay the same age.

A woman came home to find her husband in the kitchen shaking frantically, almost in a dancing frenzy, with some kind of wire running from his waist towards the electric kettle. Intending to jolt him away from the deadly current, she whacked him with a handy plank of wood, breaking his arm in two places. Up to that moment, he had been happily listening to his Walkman.

KIDS WRITE ABOUT THE SEA   1) This is a picture of an octopus. It has eight testicles. (Kelly, age 6)   2) Oysters' balls are called pearls. (James, age 6)   3) If you are surrounded by sea you are an Island. If you don't have sea all round you, you are incontinent. (Wayne, age 7)   4) Sharks are ugly and mean, and have big teeth, just like Emily Richardson. She's not my friend no more. (Kylie, age 6)   5) A dolphin breathes through an asshole on the top of its head. (Billy, age 8)   6) My uncle goes out in his boat with pots, and comes back with crabs. (Millie, age 6)   7) When ships had sails, they used to use the trade winds to cross the ocean. Sometimes, when the wind didn't blow, the sailors would whistle to make the wind come. My brother said they would have been better off   eating beans. (William, age 7)   8) I like mermaids. They are beautiful, and I like their shiny tails. And how on earth do mermaids get pregnant? Like, really? (Helen, age 6)   9) I'm not going to write about the sea. My baby brother is always screaming and being sick, my Dad keeps shouting at my Mom, and my big   sister has just got pregnant, so I can't think what to write   (Amy, age 6)   10) Some fish are dangerous. Jellyfish can sting. Electric eels can give you a shock. They have to live in caves under the sea where I think they have to plug themselves into chargers. (Christopher, age 7)   11) When you go swimming in the sea, it is very cold, and it makes my willy small.. (Kevin, age 6)   12) Divers have to be safe when they go under the water. Two divers   can't go down alone, so they have to go down on each other. (Becky, age 8)   13) On holidays my Mom went water skiing. She fell off when she was   going very fast. She says she won't do it again because water fired   right up her fat ass. (Julie, age 7)

INGENUITY

Don't just get a leg up on the competition, get 'em both up.

Two old drunks are sitting in a bar when the first one says: "Ya know, when I was thirty and got a hard-on, I couldn't bend it, even using both hands. By the time I was forty, I could bend it about ten degrees if I tried really hard. By the time I was fifty, I could bend it about twenty degrees, no problem. I'm gonna be sixty next week, and now I can bend it in half with just one hand." "So," says the second drunk, "what's your point?" "Well, I'm just wondering how much stronger I'm gonna get!"

A guy walked into the local welfare office to pick up his check. He marched straight up to the counter and said, 'Hi. You know, I just HATE drawing welfare. I'd really rather have a job.' The social worker behind the counter said, 'Your timing is excellent. We just got a job opening from a very wealthy old man who wants a chauffeur and bodyguard for his beautiful daughter. You'll have to drive around in his 2008 Mercedes-Benz CL, and he will supply all of your clothes. Because of the long hours meals will be provided. You'll also be expected to escort the daughter on her overseas holiday trips. This is rather awkward to say but you will also have as part of your job assignment to satisfy her sexual urges as the daughter is in her mid-20's and has a rather strong sex drive. A two-bedroom loft type apartment with plasma TV, stereo, bar, etc. located above the garage will be designated for your sole use and the salary is $200,000 a year.' The guy, just plain wide-eyed, said, ' You're bullshittin' me!' The social worker said, ' Yea, well... you started it.'

MOM'S MINIVAN
Less conformist than the bus.

A dad walks into a market with his young son. The kid is holding a loonie. Suddenly, the boy starts choking, going blue in the face. The dad realizes the boy has swallowed the coin and starts panicking, shouting for help. A well dressed, attractive, but serious looking woman in a blue business suit is sitting at a coffee bar in the market reading her newspaper and sipping a cup of coffee. At the sound of the commotion, she looks up, puts her coffee cup down on the saucer, neatly folds the newspaper and places it on the counter, gets up from her seat and makes her way, unhurried, across the market. Reaching the boy, the woman carefully takes hold of the boy's testicles and starts to squeeze, gently at first and then ever more firmly. After a few seconds the boy convulses violently and coughs up the coin, which the woman deftly catches in her free hand. Releasing the boy, the woman hands the coin to the father and walks back to her seat in the coffee bar without saying a word. As soon as he is sure that his son has suffered no lasting ill effects, the father rushes over to the woman and starts thanking her saying, I've never seen anybody do anything like that before, it was fantastic. Are you a doctor?   'No,' the woman replies, 'I work for Revenue Canada'

1. Part of a best friend's job should be to immediately clear your computer history if you die.
 2. Nothing sucks more than that moment during an argument when you realize you're wrong.
3.. I totally take back all those times I didn't want to nap when I was younger.
4. There is great need for a sarcasm font.
5. How the hell are you supposed to fold a fitted sheet?
6. Was learning cursive really necessary?
7. Map Quest really needs to start their directions on #5. I'm pretty sure I know how to get out of my neighborhood.
8. Obituaries would be a lot more interesting if they told you how the person died.

9. I can't remember the last time I wasn't at least kind of tired.

10. Bad decisions make good stories.

11. You never know when it will strike, but there comes a moment at work when you know that you just aren't going to do anything productive for the rest of the day.

12. Can we all just agree to ignore whatever comes after Blue Ray? I don't want to have to restart my collection...again.

13. I'm always slightly terrified when I exit out of Word and it asks me if I want to save any changes to my ten-page technical report that I swear I did not make any changes to.

14. I keep some people's phone numbers in my phone just so I know not to answer when they call.

15. I think the freezer deserves a light as well.

16. I disagree with Kay Jewelers. I would bet on any given Friday or Saturday night more kisses begin with Miller Lite than Kay.

17. I have a hard time deciphering the fine line between boredom and hunger.

18. How many times is it appropriate to say "What?" before you just nod and smile because you still didn't hear or understand a word they said?

19. I love the sense of camaraderie when an entire line of cars team up to prevent a jerk from cutting in at the front. Stay strong, brothers and sisters!

20. Shirts get dirty. Underwear gets dirty. Pants? Pants never get dirty, and you can wear them forever..

21. Sometimes I'll look down at my watch 3 consecutive times and still not know what time it is.

22. Even under ideal conditions people have trouble locating their car keys in a pocket, finding their cell phone, and Pinning the Tail on the Donkey - but I'd bet everyone can find and push the snooze button from 3 feet away, in about 1.7 seconds, eyes closed, first time, every time.

23. The first testicular guard, the "Cup," was used in Hockey in 1874 and the first helmet was used in 1974. That means it only took 100 years for men to realize that their brain is also important.

FATHERHOOD

If you kill that hooker, you can get your money back

Sitting together on a train, traveling through the Canadian Rockies, were a fellow from British Columbia, A fellow from Quebec, a little old Greek lady, and a young blonde girl with large breasts. The train goes into a dark tunnel and a few seconds later there is the sound of a loud slap. When the train emerges from the tunnel, the fellow from Quebec has a bright red hand print on his cheek. No one speaks. The little old Greek lady thinks: The fellow from Quebec must has groped the blonde in the dark and she slapped his cheek.
  The blonde girl thinks: That fellow from Quebec must have tried to grope me in the dark, but missed and fondled the old lady and she slapped his cheek. The fellow from Quebec thinks: That fellow from British Columbia must have groped the blonde in the dark. She tried to slap him but missed and got me instead. The fellow from British Columbia thinks: I can't wait for another tunnel, just so I can smack the fellow from Quebec again. Now THAT'S a Western Canadian!

VAGINA

It's not a clown car.

God went to the A-rabs and said 'I have Commandments for you that will make your lives better.'

The Arabs asked, 'What are Commandments?' And the Lord said, 'There are rules for living.'

'Can you give us an example?' 'Thou shall not kill. 'Not kill?   We're not interested.' So He went to the Blacks and said, 'I have Commandments.' The Blacks wanted an example, and the Lord said, 'Honour thy Father and Mother.' 'Father? We don't know who our fathers are.   We're not interested.' Then He went to the Mexicans and said, 'I have Commandments.' The Mexicans also wanted an example, and the Lord said 'Thou shall not steal.' 'Not steal?   We're not interested.' Then He went to the French and said, 'I have Commandments.' The French too wanted an example and the Lord said, 'Thou shall not commit adultery.'

'Not commit adultery?   We're not interested.' Finally, He went to the Jews and said, 'I have commandments.' 'Commandments?' They said, 'How much are they?' 'They're free.' 'We'll take 10.'

There, that should offend just about everybody.

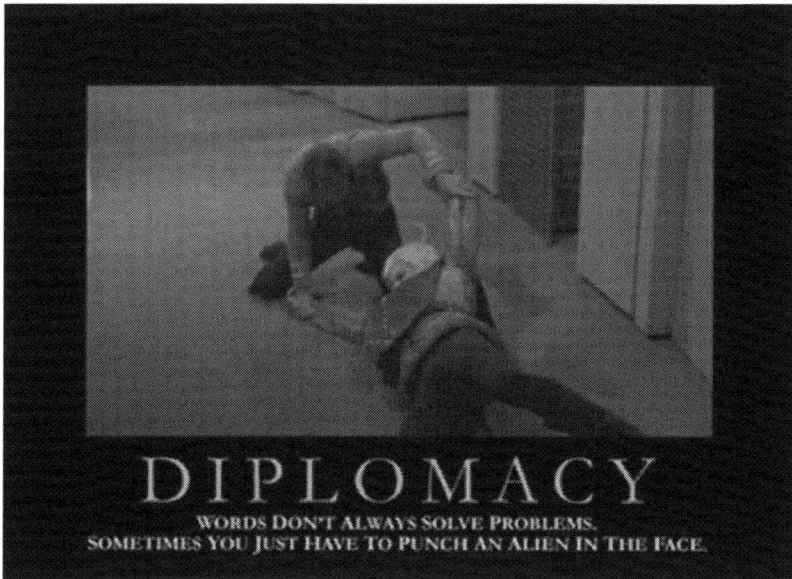

DIPLOMACY
WORDS DON'T ALWAYS SOLVE PROBLEMS.
SOMETIMES YOU JUST HAVE TO PUNCH AN ALIEN IN THE FACE.

A girl comes up to a guy at the party and says, "My name is Carmen because those are the two things I like best in the world. The fast thinking guy says, "Pleased to meet you, my name is Beertits.

Husband: 'When I get mad at you, you never fight back. How do you control your anger?'   Wife: 'I clean the toilet.'   Husband: 'How does that help?'   Wife: 'I use your toothbrush.'

After numerous rounds of "We don't even know if Osama is still alive", Osama himself decided to send George Bush a letter in his own handwriting to let him know he was still in the game.   Bush opened the letter and it contained a single line of coded message: 370H-SSV-0773H   Bush was baffled, so he showed it to Condoleezza Rice. Condi and her aides had not a clue either, so they sent it to the FBI. No one could solve it at the FBI so it went to the CIA, then to MI6 and Mossad.
   Eventually they asked the Royal Canadian Mounted Police for help. Within a minute the RCMP emailed the White House with this reply: 'Tell the president he's holding the message upside down'.

A woman in her fifties went to a plastic surgeon for a facelift. The surgeon told her about a new procedure called "The Knob,"where a small knob is placed on the top of a woman's head and can be turned to tighten up her skin to produce the effect of a brand new facelift. Of course the woman wanted "The Knob."

Over the course of the years, the woman tightened the knob and the effects were wonderful. The woman remained young looking and vibrant.

After fifteen years, the woman returned to the surgeon with two problems.

"All of these years, everything has been working just fine. I have turned the knob many times and have been very pleased with the results. But now, I've developed two annoying problems:

First, I have these terrible bags under my eyes and the knob won't get rid of them."

The doctor looked at her closely and said, "Those aren't bags, those are your breasts."

She said, "Well, I guess there's no point in asking about the goatee!"

The average cost of rehabilitating a seal after the Exxon Valdez Oil spill in Alaska was $80,000.00 At a special ceremony, two of the most expensively saved animals were being released back into the wild amid cheers and applause from onlookers. A minute later, in full view, a killer whale ate them both.

Did you know that in the human body there is a nerve that connects the eyeball to the anus? It's called the Anal Optic Nerve, and it is responsible for giving people a shitty outlook on life. If you don't believe it, pull a hair from your ass and see if it doesn't bring a tear to your eyes.

Red Neck Calamari

I was a very happy person. My wonderful girlfriend and I had been dating for over a year, and so we decided to get married. There was only one little thing bothering me...It was her beautiful younger sister.

My prospective sister-in-law was twenty-two, wore very tight miniskirts, and generally was bra-less. She would regularly bend down when she was near me, and I always got more than a pleasant view of her private parts. It had to be deliberate. She never did it when she was near anyone else. One day her little" sister called and asked me to come over to check the wedding invitations. She was alone when I arrived, and she whispered to me that she had feelings and desires for me that she couldn't overcome. She told me that she wanted to make love to me just once before I got married and committed my life to her sister. Well, I was in total shock, and couldn't say a word. She said, "I'm going upstairs to my bedroom, and if you want one last wild fling, just come up and get me."

I was stunned and frozen in shock as I watched her go up the stairs. When she reached the top she pulled off her panties and threw them down the stairs at me. I stood there for a moment, then turned and made a beeline straight to the front door. I opened the door, and headed straight towards my car.

Lo and behold, my entire future family was standing outside, all clapping! With tears in his eyes, my father-in-law hugged me and said, "We are very happy that you have passed our little test. We couldn't ask for a better man for our daughter. Welcome to the family."

And the moral of this story is: Always keep your condoms in your car.

Economic Models explained with cows

SOCIALISM You have 2 cows. You give one to your neighbour.

COMMUNISM You have 2 cows. The State takes both and gives you some milk.   FASCISM You have 2 cows. The State takes both and sells you some milk.

NAZISM You have 2 cows. The State takes both and shoots you.   BUREAUCRATISM You have 2 cows. The State takes both, shoots one, milks the other, and then throws the milk away...   TRADITIONAL CAPITALISM You have two cows. You sell one and buy a bull. Your herd multiplies, and the economy grows. You sell them and retire on the income.

SURREALISM You have two giraffes. The government requires you to take harmonica lessons

AN AMERICAN CORPORATION You have two cows. You sell one, and force the other to produce the milk of four cows. Later, you hire a consultant to analyse why the cow has dropped dead.

ENRON VENTURE CAPITALISM You have two cows. You sell three of them to your publicly listed company, using letters of credit opened by your brother-in-law at the bank, then execute a debt/equity swap with an associated general offer so that you get all four cows back, with a tax exemption for five cows. The milk rights of the six cows are transferred via an intermediary to a Cayman Island Company secretly owned by the majority shareholder who sells the rights to all seven cows back to your listed company. The annual report says the company owns eight cows, with an option on one more. You sell one cow to buy a new president of the United States, leaving you with nine cows. No balance sheet provided with the release. The public then buys your bull.

A FRENCH CORPORATION You have two cows. You go on strike, organise a riot, and block the roads, because you want three cows.

A JAPANESE CORPORATION You have two cows. You redesign them so they are one-tenth the size of an ordinary cow and produce twenty times the milk. You then create a clever cow cartoon image called 'Cowkimon' and market it worldwide.

A GERMAN CORPORATION You have two cows. You re-engineer them so they live for 100 years, eat once a month, and milk themselves.

AN ITALIAN CORPORATION You have two cows, but you don't know where they are. You decide to have lunch.

A RUSSIAN CORPORATION You have two cows. You count them and learn you have five cows. You count them again and learn you have 42 cows. You count them again and learn you have 2 cows. You stop counting cows and open another bottle of vodka.

A SWISS CORPORATION You have 5000 cows. None of them belong to you. You charge the owners for storing them.

A CHINESE CORPORATION You have two cows. You have 300 people milking them. You claim that you have full employment, and high bovine productivity. You arrest the newsman who reported the real situation.

AN INDIAN CORPORATION You have two cows. You worship them.

A BRITISH CORPORATION You have two cows. Both are mad.

AN IRAQI CORPORATION Everyone thinks you have lots of cows. You tell them that you have none. No-one believes you, so they bomb you and invade your country. You still have no cows, but at least now you are part of a Democracy....

AN AUSTRALIAN CORPORATION You have two cows. Business seems pretty good. You close the office and go for a few beers to celebrate.

A NEW ZEALAND CORPORATION You have two cows. The one on the left looks very attractive

The scientific theory I like best is that the rings of Saturn are composed entirely of lost airline baggage

An old pilot is one who can remember when flying was dangerous and sex was safe

Both optimists and pessimists contribute to the society. The optimist invents the aeroplane, the pessimist the parachute.

Airlines have really changed; now a flight attendant can get a pilot pregnant.

If helicopters are so safe, how come there are no vintage/classic helicopter fly-ins

Death is just nature's way of telling you to watch your airspeed or rotor RPM

Real planes use only a single stick to fly. This is why bulldozers & helicopters -- in that order -- need two.'

There are only three things the copilot should ever say:
1. Nice landing, Sir.
2. I'll buy the first round.
3. I'll take the ugly one.

As a pilot, only two bad things can happen to you and one of them will.
a. One day you will walk out to the aircraft knowing that it is your last flight.
b. One day you will walk out to the aircraft not knowing that it is your last flight.

EASTER
Don't bother looking for eggs.

There are Rules and there are Laws. The Rules are made by men who think that they know how to fly your airplane better than you.

Laws (of Physics) are made by the Great One. You can, and sometimes should, suspend the Rules but you can never suspend the Laws.

About Rules:

a. The rules are a good place to hide if you don't have a better idea and the talent to execute it.

b. If you deviate from a rule, it must be a flawless performance. (e.g., If you fly under a bridge, don't hit the bridge).

The ideal pilot is the perfect blend of discipline and aggressiveness.

To become a jet pilot, one must be an egomaniac with low self esteem.

The medical profession is the natural enemy of the aviation profession.

Ever notice that the only experts who decree that the age of the pilot is over are people who have never flown anything? Also, in spite of the intensity of their feelings that the pilot's day is over I know of no expert who has volunteered to be a passenger in a non-piloted aircraft.

Before each flight, make sure that your bladder is empty and your fuel tanks are full!

He who demands everything that his aircraft can give him is a pilot; he that demands one iota more is a fool.

There are certain aircraft sounds that can only be heard at night.

The aircraft limits are only there in case there is another flight by that particular aircraft. If subsequent flights do not appear likely, there are no limits.

Flying is a great way of life for men who want to feel like boys, but not for those who still are.

Flying is a hard way to earn an easy living.

Forget all that stuff about lift, gravity, thrust and drag. An airplane flies because of money. If God had meant man to fly, He'd have given him more money.

If black boxes survive air crashes -- why don't they make the whole plane out of that stuff?

'If the Wright brothers were alive today Wilbur would have to fire Orville to reduce costs.' President DELTA Airlines

In the Alaska bush I'd rather have a two hour bladder and three hours of gas than vice versa.

It's not that all airplane pilots are good-looking. Its Just that good-looking people seem more capable of flying airplanes. Or so seasoned observers contend. A matter of self-confidence? No doubt, no doubt.

I've flown in both pilot seats, can someone tell me why the other one is always occupied by an idiot?

Son, you're going to have to make up your mind about growing up and becoming a pilot. You can't do both.

There are only two types of aircraft -- fighters and targets.

You define a good flight by negatives: you didn't get hijacked, you didn't crash, you didn't throw up, you weren't late, and you weren't nauseated by the food. So you're grateful.

  New FAA Motto: We're not happy, till you're not happy.

An old pilot sat down at the bar and ordered a drink.
As he sat sipping his drink, a young woman sat down next to him. She turned to the old pilot who had his old goggles round his neck, was reading an old copy of Flight Deck and drinking Horses Neck, and asked, "Are you a real pilot?"
He replied, "Well, I've spent my whole life flying fighters and helicopters and everything in between, had accidents, flown off ships and in the jungle, desert and so on, so I suppose you could say that I am a real pilot"

She said, "I'm a lesbian. I spend my whole day thinking about women. As soon as I get up in the morning, I think about women. When I shower, I think about women. When I watch TV, I think about women. I even think about women when I eat. It seems that everything makes me think of women."
The two sat sipping in silence.
A little while later, a man sat down on the other side of the old pilot and asked, "Are you a real pilot?" He replied, "I always thought I was but I just found out I'm a lesbian.

When I got home last night, my wife demanded that I take her someplace expensive.... so, I took her to a gas station....and that's when my lights suddenly went out....

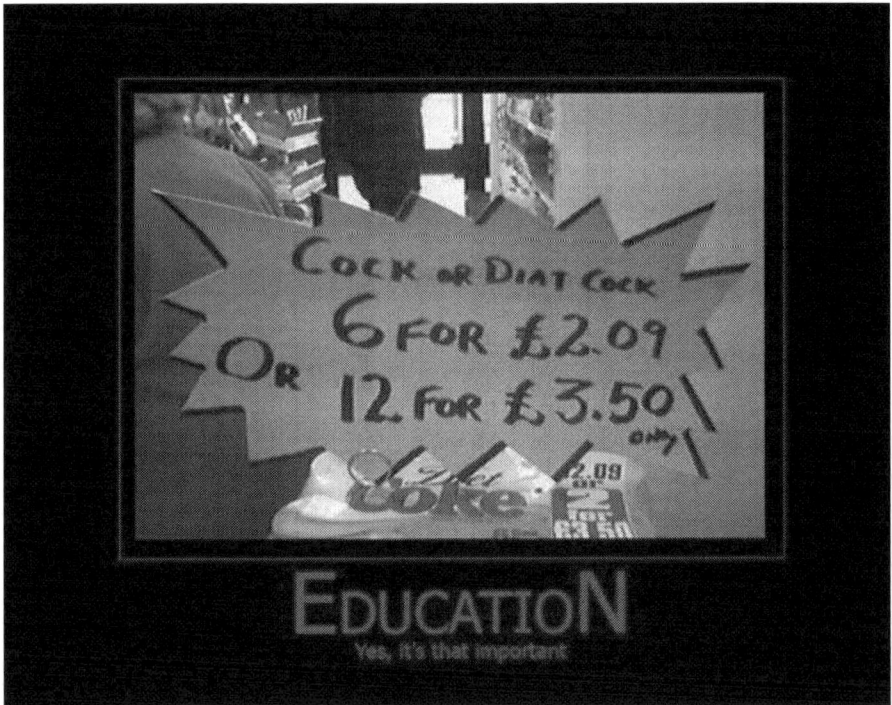

THINGS THAT ARE DIFFICULT TO SAY WHEN YOU'RE DRUNK:
Indubitably

Innovative
Preliminary
Proliferation
Cinnamon

THINGS THAT ARE VERY DIFFICULT TO SAY WHEN
YOU'RE DRUNK:
Specificity
British Constitution
Loquacious Transubstantiate

THINGS THAT ARE DOWNRIGHT IMPOSSIBLE TO SAY
WHEN YOU'RE DRUNK:
Thanks, but I don't want to have sex.
Nope, no more booze for me.
Sorry, but you're not really my type.
Good evening officer isn't it lovely out tonight.
Oh, I just couldn't....No one wants to hear me sing

A man walks into his bedroom with a sheep under his arm.
His wife is lying in bed, reading.
"This is the pig I have sex with when you've got a headache."
"I think you'll find that's a sheep," says his wife.
"And I think you'll find," says the man, "that I was talking to
the sheep."

All Grandpas Should Heed This Warning:
Whatever you do, do NOT lose your Grand kids in the
Shopping Mall.
A small boy was lost at a large shopping mall. He approached
a uniformed
policeman and said, "I've lost my grandpa!"
The cop asked, "What's he like?"
The little boy hesitated for a moment and then replied, "Jim
Beam and ladies with big tits".

Guts or Balls...

There is a medical distinction. We've all heard about people having guts or balls, but do you really know the difference between them?. In an effort to keep you informed, the definitions are listed below:

GUTS - Is arriving home late after a night out with the boys, being met by your wife with a broom, and having the guts to ask: "Are you still cleaning, or are you flying somewhere?".

BALLS - Is coming home late after a night out with the boys, smelling of perfume and beer, lipstick on your collar, slapping your wife on the arse and having the balls to say: "You're next, fatty".

I hope this clears up any confusion on the definitions. Medically speaking, there is no difference in the outcome, since both ultimately result in death.

A man kills a deer and takes it home to cook for dinner. Both he and his wife decide that they won't tell the kids what kind of meat it is, but will give them a clue and let them guess. The kids were eager to know what the meat was on their plates, so begged their dad for the clue. "Well" the father said, "It's what mummy calls me sometimes"The little girl screams, "Don't eat it.... its a f#@king asshole!

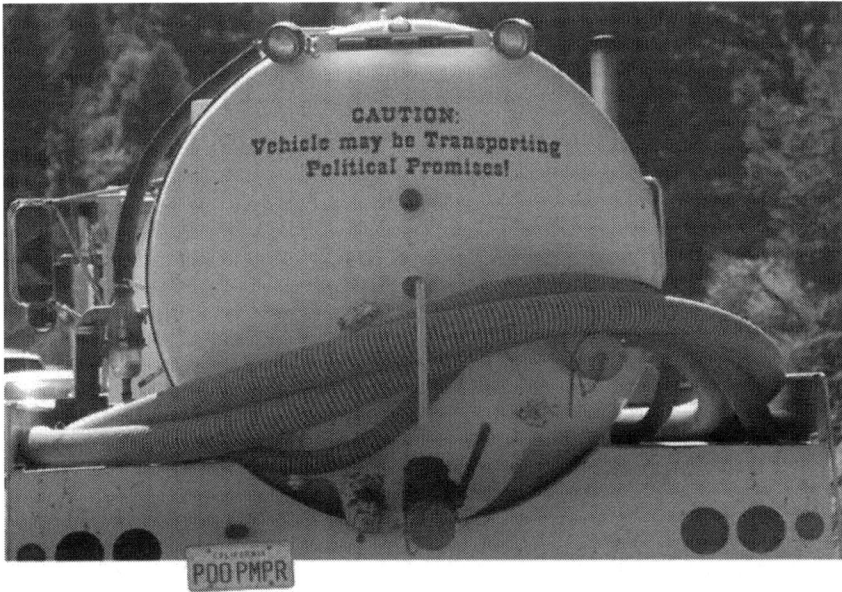

CAUTION:
Vehicle may be Transporting
Political Promises!

PDO PMPR

What is a Yankee? The same as a quickie, but a guy can do it alone.

What is the difference between a Harley and a Hoover? The position of the dirt bag

Why is divorce so expensive? Because it's worth it.

What do you see when the Pillsbury Dough Boy bends over? Doughnuts

Why is air a lot like sex? Because it's no big deal unless you're not getting any.

What do you call a smart blonde? A golden retriever.

What do attorneys use for birth control? Their personalities.

What's the difference between a girlfriend and wife? 10 years and 45 lbs

What's the difference between a boyfriend and husband? 45 minutes

What's the fastest way to a man's heart? Through his chest with a sharp knife

Why do men want to marry virgins? They can't stand criticism.

Why is it so hard for women to find men that are sensitive, caring, and good-looking? Because those men already have boyfriends.

What's the difference between a new husband and a new dog? After a year, the dog is still excited to see you

Why do men chase women they have no intention of marrying? The same urge that makes dogs chase cars they have no intention of driving.

Why don't bunnies make noise when they have sex? Because they have cotton balls.

What's the difference between a porcupine and BMW? A porcupine has the pricks on the outside.

What did the blonde say when she found out she was pregnant? 'Are you sure it's mine?'

Why does Mike Tyson cry during sex? Mace will do that to you.

Why did OJ Simpson want to move to West Virginia? Everyone has the same DNA.

Why do drivers' education classes in Redneck schools use the car only on Mondays, Wednesdays and Fridays? Because on Tuesday and Thursday, the Sex Ed class uses it.

Where does an Irish family go on vacation? A different bar.

Did you hear about the Chinese couple that had a Blonde baby? They named him 'Sum Ting Wong'

What would you call it when an Italian has one arm shorter than the other? A speech impediment

What's the difference between a southern zoo and a northern zoo? A southern zoo has a description of the animal on the front of the cage along with... 'A recipe'.

How do you get a sweet 80-year-old lady to say the F word? Get another sweet little 80-year-old lady to yell *BINGO*!

What's the difference between a northern fairytale and a southern fairytale? A northern fairytale begins 'Once upon a time..' -A southern fairytale begins 'Y'all ain't gonna believe this S**t....

Sometimes, when I look at my children, I say to myself 'Barbara, you should have remained a virgin. -- Barbara Bush

I had a rose named after me and I was very flattered. But I was not pleased to read the description in the catalog: 'No good in a bed, but fine against a wall.'   -- Eleanor Roosevelt

Last week, I stated this woman was the ugliest woman I had ever seen. I have since been visited by her sister, and now wish to withdraw that statement -- Mark Twain

The secret of a good sermon is to have a good beginning and a good ending; and to have the two as close together as possible. -- George Burns

 Santa Claus has the right idea. Visit people only once a year- - Victor Borge

Be careful about reading health books. You may die of a misprint-- Mark Twain

By all means, marry. If you get a good wife, you'll become happy; if you get a bad one, you'll become a philosopher. -- Socrates

I was married by a judge. I should have asked for a jury-- Groucho Marx

I never drink water because of the disgusting things that fish do in it.   -- W.C Fields

We could certainly slow the aging process down if it had to work its way through Congress - Will Rogers

Don't worry about avoiding temptation as you grow older, it will avoid you.   -- Winston Churchill

By the time a man is wise enough to watch his step, he's too old to go anywhere.   ---Billy Crystal

The cardiologist's diet: If it tastes good, spit it out.

NEW OFFICE POLICY

Dress Code:

1) You are advised to come to work dressed according to your salary.

2) If we see you wearing Prada shoes and carrying a Gucci bag, we will assume you are doing well financially and therefore do not need a raise.

3) If you dress poorly, you need to learn to manage your money better, so that you may buy nicer clothes, and therefore you do not need a raise.

4) If you dress just right, you are right where you need to be and therefore you do not need a raise.

Sick Days:
We will no longer accept a doctor's statement as proof of sickness. If you are able to go to the doctor, you are able to come to work.

Personal Days:
Each employee will receive 104 personal days a year. They are called Saturdays & Sundays.

Bathroom Breaks:
Entirely too much time is being spent in the toilet. There is now a strict three-minute time limit in the stalls. At the end of three minutes, an alarm will sound, the toilet paper roll will retract, the stall door will open, and a picture will be taken.
 After your second offense, your picture will be posted on the company bulletin board under the 'Chronic Offenders' category. Anyone caught smiling in the picture will be sectioned under the company's mental health policy.

Lunch Break:

* Skinny people get 30 minutes for lunch, as they need to eat more, so that they can look healthy.

* Normal size people get 15 minutes for lunch to get a balanced meal to maintain their average figure.

* Chubby people get 5 minutes for lunch, because that's all the time needed to drink a Slim-Fast.

Thank you for your loyalty to our company.   Never forget that we are here to provide a positive employment experience. Therefore, all questions, comments, concerns, complaints, frustrations, irritations, aggravations, insinuations, allegations, accusations, contemplations, consternation and input should be directed elsewhere.

A duck walks into a pub and orders a pint of beer and a ham sandwich. The barman looks at him and says, "Hang on! You're a duck." "I see your eyes are working," replies the duck. "And you can talk!" exclaims the barman. "I see your ears are working, too," says the duck. "Now if you don't mind, can I have my beer and my sandwich please?" "Certainly, sorry about that," says the barman as he pulls the duck's pint. "It's just we don't get many ducks in this pub. What are you doing round this way?" "I'm working on the building site across the road," explains the duck. "I'm a dry-waller." The flabbergasted barman cannot believe the duck and wants to learn more, but takes the hint when the duck pulls out a newspaper from his bag and proceeds to read it. So, the duck reads his paper, drinks his beer, eats his sandwich, bids the barman good day and leaves.

The same thing happens for two weeks. Then one day the circus comes to town. The ringmaster comes into the pub for a pint and the barman says to him "You're with the circus, aren't you? Well, I know this duck that could be just brilliant in your circus. He talks, drinks beer, eats sandwiches, reads the newspaper and everything!" "Sounds marvellous," says the ringmaster, handing over his business card. "Get him to give me a call." So the next day when the duck comes into the pub the barman says, "Hey Mr. Duck, I reckon I can line you up with a top job, paying really good money." "I'm always looking for the next job," says the duck. "Where is it?" "At the circus," says the barman. "The circus?" repeats the duck.

 "That's right," replies the barman. "The circus?" the duck asks again. "That place with the big tent?" "Yeah," the barman replies. "With all the animals who live in cages and performers who live in caravans?" says the duck. "Of course," the barman replies. "And the tent has canvas sides and a big canvas roof with a hole in the middle?" persists the duck.

 "That's right!" says the barman. The duck shakes his head in amazement, and says.... "What the fuck would they want with a dry waller?"

A dog is truly a man's best friend. If you don't believe it, just try this experiment. Put your dog and your wife in the trunk of the car for an hour. When you open the trunk, who is really happy to see you?

How to be cruel to old guys with bad vision...

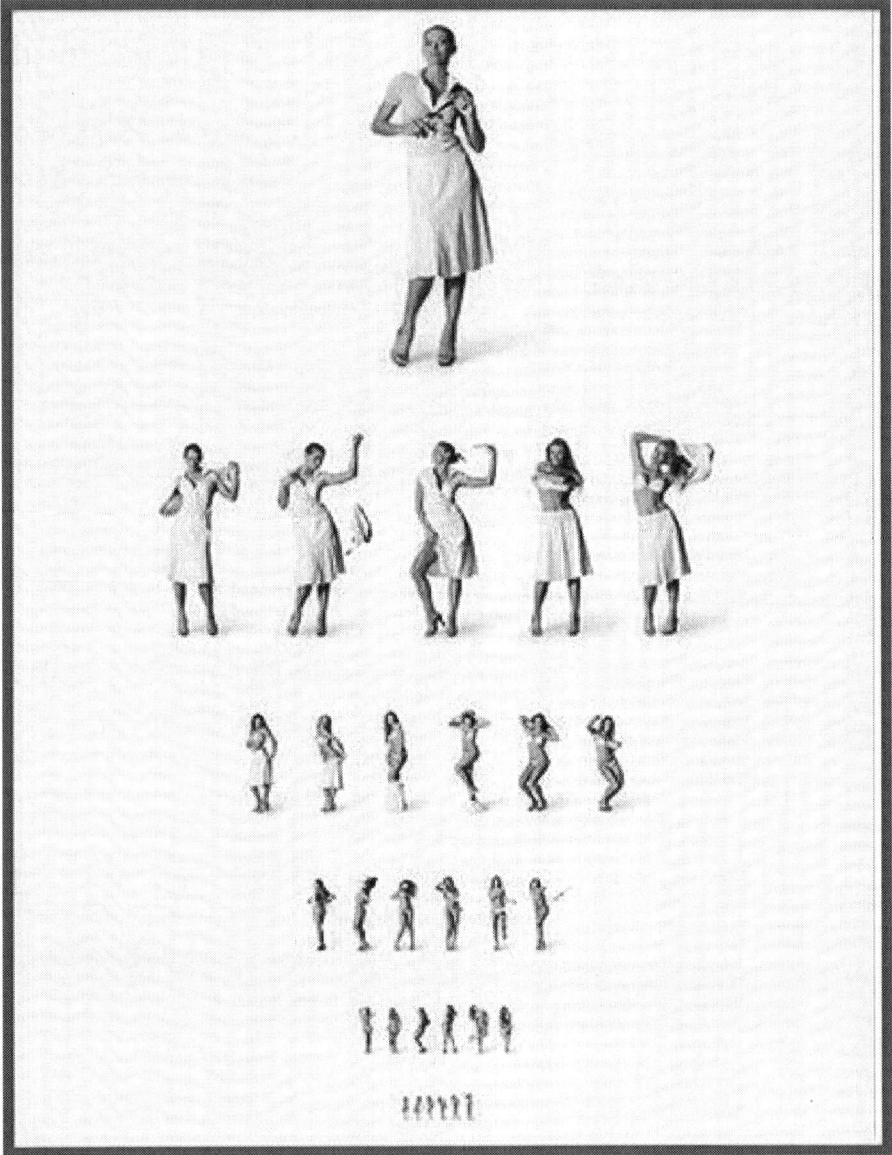

1. The roundest knight at king Arthur's round table was Sir Cumference. He acquired his size from too much pi.

2. I thought I saw an eye doctor on an Alaskan island,
   but it turned out to be an optical Aleutian .

3. She was only a whisky maker,
   but he loved her still.

4. A rubber band pistol was confiscated from algebra class because
   it was a weapon of math disruption.

5. The butcher backed into the meat grinder
   and got a little behind in his work.

6. No matter how much you push the envelope,
   it'll still be stationery.

7. A dog gave birth to puppies near the road
   and was cited for littering.

8. A grenade thrown into a kitchen in France would result in
   Linoleum Blownapart.

9. Two silk worms had a race.
   They ended up in a tie.

10. Time flies like an arrow.
    Fruit flies like a banana.

11. A hole has been found in the nudist camp wall.
    The police are looking into it.

12. Atheism is a non-prophet organization.

13. Two hats were hanging on a hat rack in the hallway.
    One hat said to the other, 'You stay here, I'll go on a head.'

14. I wondered why the baseball kept getting bigger.
   Then it hit me.

15. A sign on the lawn at a drug rehab center said: 'Keep off the Grass.'

16. A small boy swallowed some coins and was taken to a hospital.
   When his grandmother telephoned to ask how he was, a nurse said, 'No change yet.'

17. A chicken crossing the road is poultry in motion.

18. It's not that the man did not know how to juggle, he just didn't have the balls to do it.

19. The short fortune-teller who escaped from prison was a small medium at large.

20. The man who survived mustard gas and pepper spray is now a seasoned veteran.

21. A backward poet writes inverse.

22. In democracy it's your vote that counts.
   In feudalism it's your count that votes.

23. When cannibals ate a missionary, they got a taste of religion.

On their wedding night, the young bride Approached her new Husband and asked for $20.00 for their first Lovemaking encounter. In His highly aroused state, her husband readily Agreed. This scenario was repeated each time they made Love, for more Than 30 years, with him thinking that it was a Cute way for her to Afford new clothes and other incidentals that She needed. Arriving home around noon one day, she was Surprised to find Her husband in a very drunken state. During the next few minutes, he explained that His employer Was going through a process of corporate Downsizing, and he had Been let go. It was unlikely that, at the age of 59, he'd be able to find Another position that paid anywhere near what He'd been earning, and Therefore, they Were financially ruined. Calmly, his wife handed him a bank book which Showed more than thirty Years of steady deposits and interest totaling Nearly $1 million. Then she showed him certificates of deposits issued by the bank which were worth over $2 million, And informed him that they were one of the largest depositors in the bank. She explained that for the more than three decades she had 'charged' him for sex, these holdings had multiplied And these were the Results of her savings and investments. Faced with evidence of cash and investments Worth over $3 Million, her husband was so astounded he could barely speak, but finally he found his voice and blurted out, 'If I'd had any idea what you were doing, I would have given you all my Business!' That's when she shot him. You know, sometimes, men just don't know when to keep their mouths shut

When you discover you are riding a dead horse the best strategy is to dismount.

Did you hear about the blonde who called her zebra Spot?

Advertising is the price companies pay for being unoriginal.

Hung Chow calls into work and says, 'Hey, I no come work today, I really sick. Got headache, stomach ache and legs hurt, I no come work.'The boss says, 'You know something, Hung Chow, I really need you today. When I feel sick like you do, I go to my wife and tell her to give me Sex. That Makes everything better and I go to work. You try that.'Two hours later Hung Chow calls again. 'I do what You say and I feel Great. I be at work soon.........You got nice house'

A man was laying in bed with his new girlfriend. After having great sex, she spent the next hour just scratching his nuts - something she seemed to love to do. As he was enjoying it, he turned and asked her, 'Why do you love doing that?" Because,' she replied, 'I really miss mine.'

'Life's tough.....it's even tougher if you're stupid." -- John Wayne

In George Washington's days, there were no cameras. One's image was either sculpted or painted. Some paintings of George Washington showed him standing behind a desk with one arm behind his back while others showed both legs and both arms. Prices charged by painters were not based on how many people were to be painted, but by how many limbs were to be painted. Arms and legs are 'limbs,' therefore painting them would cost the buyer more.. Hence the expression, 'Okay, but it'll cost you an arm and a leg.' (Artists know hands and arms are more difficult to paint)

A young boy enters a barbershop and the barber whispers to his customer, "This is the dumbest kid in the world. Watch while I prove it."

The barber puts a dollar bill in one hand and two quarters in the other, then calls the boy over and asks, "Which do you want, son?"

The boy takes the quarters and leaves the dollar.

"What did I tell you?" said the barber. "That kid never learns!"

Later, the customer leaves, and sees the same young boy coming out of the ice cream store. He asks. "Hey, son! May I ask you a question? Why did you take the quarters instead of the dollar bill?"

The boy licked his cone and replied, "Because the day I take the dollar, the game's over!"

An elderly couple was attending church services. About halfway through, she leaned over and whispered to her husband, 'I just let out a long silent fart. What do you think I should do?' He replied, 'Put a new battery in your hearing aid.'

FIVE RULES FOR MEN TO FOLLOW TO A HAPPY LIFE: 1. It's important to have a woman, who helps at home, Who cooks from time to time, cleans up and has a job. 2. It's important to have a woman, who can make you Laugh. 3. It's important to have a woman, who you can trust And who doesn't lie to you. 4. It's important to have a woman, who is good in bed And who likes to be with you. 5. It's very, very important that these four women Do not know each other.

A lesson to be learned from typing the wrong email address! A Minneapolis couple decided to go to Florida to thaw out during a particularly icy winter. They planned to stay at the same hotel where they spent their honeymoon 20 years earlier.

Because of hectic schedules, it was difficult to coordinate their travel schedules. So, the husband left Minnesota and flew to Florida on Thursday, with his wife flying down the following day. The husband checked into the hotel. There was a computer in his room, so he decided to send an email to his wife. However, he accidentally left out one letter in her email address, and without realizing his error, sent the email.

Meanwhile, somewhere in Houston, a widow had just returned home from her husband's funeral. He was a minister who was called home to glory following a heart attack.

The widow decided to check her email expecting messages from relatives and friends. After reading the first message, she screamed and fainted.

The widow's son rushed into the room, found his mother on the floor, and saw the computer screen which read:

To: My Loving Wife
Subject: I've Arrived
Date: October 16, 2007

I know you're surprised to hear from me. They have computers here now and you are allowed to send emails to your loved ones.

I've just arrived and have been checked in. I see that everything has been prepared for your arrival tomorrow. Looking forward to seeing you then! Hope your journey is as uneventful as mine was.

P.S. Sure is freaking hot down here!

If you don't like it - it is fake. If you do like it it is faux.

Guy says to his wife:
"Darling, what would you do if I said I've won the lottery?"
Wife replies: "Id take half then leave you."
Guy says: "Excellent! I had three numbers and won ten dollars. Here's a fiver- now fuck off!

For every mile of road there are two miles of ditch.

232

MARRIAGE
Better Start Drinking Now, It Only Gets Worse From Here

In 1 day... How can 2 million African-Americans get into Washington DC in
sub-zero temps with bridges closed under tight security in the biggest
traffic jam in American history....when 200,000 couldn't get out of New
Orleans at 85 degrees with four days notice?

If a man tries to fail and succeeds, which did he do?

Woman strips naked and rolls dice "I won" she says and takes the winnings. "What did she roll?" asks one dealer. "I don't know I thought you were watching," says the other.

Three women are in a locker room dressing to play tennis when a man runs through wearing only a bag on his head. The first woman looks at his penis and says, "Well, it's not my husband." The second woman says "No it isn't." The third says, "He's not even a member of this club."

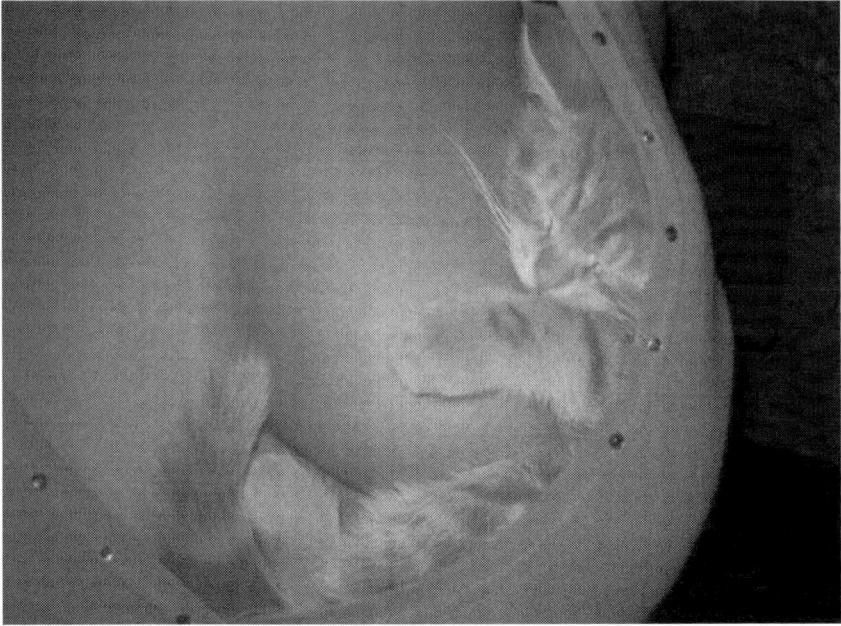

A man entered the bus with both of his front pockets full of golf balls and sat down next to a beautiful (you guessed it) blonde. The puzzled blonde kept looking at him and his bulging pockets. Finally, after many such glances from her, he said, "It's golf balls". Nevertheless, the blonde continued to look at him for a very long time, deeply thinking about what he had said. After several minutes, not being able to contain her curiosity any longer, asked, "Does it hurt as much as tennis elbow?"

WTF

Seriously, WTF is that???

www.so-easy.uni.cc

Little Red Riding Hood is skipping down the road when she sees a Big bad wolf crouched down behind a log. ' My, what big eyes you have, Mr. Wolf.' The wolf jumps up and runs away. Further down the road Little Red Riding Hood sees the wolf again, and this time he is crouched behind a bush. ' My, what big ears you have, Mr. Wolf.' Again the wolf jumps up and runs away. About a half mile down the road Little Red Riding Hood sees the Wolf again, and this time he is crouched down behind a rock. 'My, what big teeth you have, Mr. Wolf.' With that the wolf jumps up and screams, 'Will you fuckoff? I'm trying to have a shit.'

Never confuse brains with a bull market.

East Indian traffic accident victims - Bin Dunder Jeep, Banged la Dash. Travel Agent - Bin Dere Done Da

WAR FACE

You can be wearing a life jacket and gardening gloves to a war and still look badass

Recently I was asked to play in a golf tournament. At first I said, 'Naaahhh!' Then they said to me 'Come on, it's for handicapped and blind Kids.' Then I thought... Fuck - I could win this!'

A New York boy is being led through the swamps of Louisiana by his cousin. "Is it true that an alligator won't attack you if you carry a flashlight?" asks the city boy. His cousin replies, "Depends on how fast you carry the flashlight."

Life is a sexually transmitted disease with 100% chance of mortality.

An optimist thinks this is the best of all possible worlds. A pessimist fears this is so.

A man is cupping his hand to scoop water from a Highland burn. A Gamekeeper shouts, 'Dinnae drink tha waater! Et's foo ae coo's sheet an pish!' The man replies, 'My Good fellow, I'm from England. Could you repeat that in English for me' The keeper replies, 'I said, use two hands - you spill less that way!

An Irishman walks into a bar and orders 3 pints. "Why not one at a time?" asks the bartender. "I am drinking with my brothers who are away working in America. We promised we would do it this way." One day he walks in and orders only 2. A hush falls among the regulars and the bar tender says, "Please accept my condolences." The Irishman says " Oh no. Everyone is all right. It is just that I have joined the Mormon Church and have had to quit drinking."

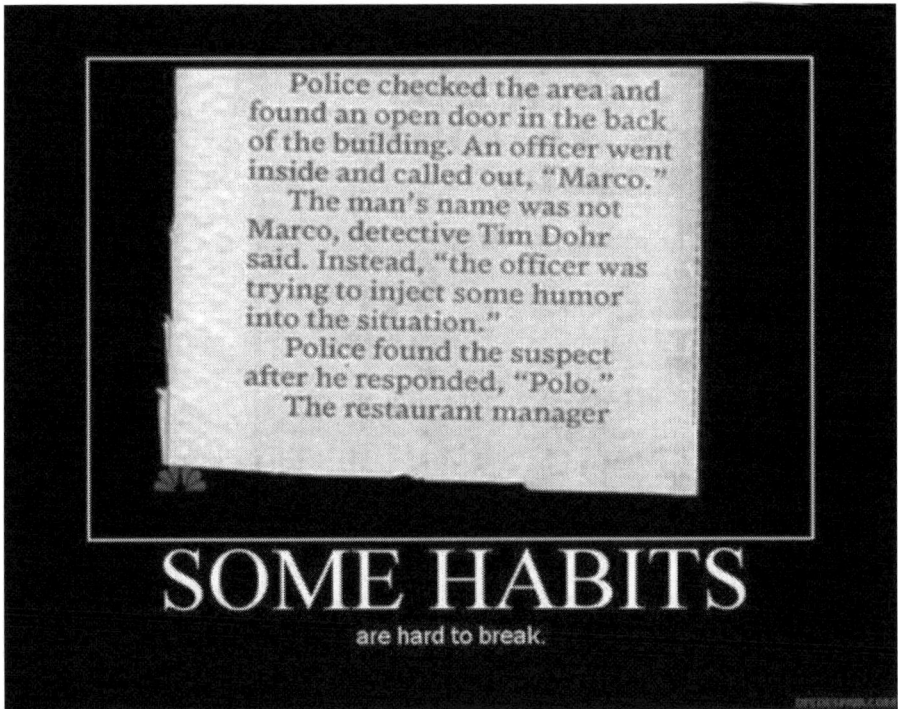

Police checked the area and found an open door in the back of the building. An officer went inside and called out, "Marco."
    The man's name was not Marco, detective Tim Dohr said. Instead, "the officer was trying to inject some humor into the situation."
    Police found the suspect after he responded, "Polo."
    The restaurant manager

SOME HABITS
are hard to break.

What do you get when you mix PMS with GPS? A crazy bitch who <u>will</u> find you

Homer Simpson look alike contest winner...

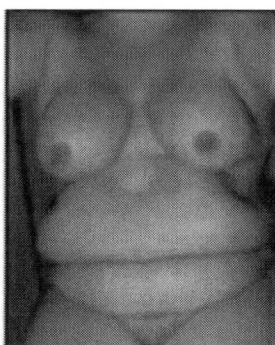

1 - I'd kill for a Nobel Peace Prize.

2 - Borrow money from pessimists. They don't expect it back.

3 - Half the people you know are below average.

4 - 99% of lawyers give the rest a bad name.

5 - 82.7% of all statistics are made up on the spot.

6 - A conscience is what hurts when all your other parts feel so good.

7 - A clear conscience is usually the sign of a bad memory.

8 - If you want the rainbow, you got to put up with the rain.

9 - All those who believe in psycho-kinesis, raise my hand.

10 - The early bird may get the worm, but the second mouse gets the cheese.

11 - I almost had a psychic girl friend, but she left me before we met.

12 - OK, so what's the speed of dark?

13 - How do you tell when you're out of invisible ink?

14 - If everything seems to be going well, you have obviously overlooked something.

15 - Depression is merely anger without enthusiasm.

16 - When everything is coming your way, you're in the wrong lane.

17 - Ambition is a poor excuse for not having enough sense to be lazy.

18 - Hard work pays off in the future, laziness pays off now.

19 - I intend to live forever. So far, so good.

20 - If Barbie is so popular, why do you have to buy her friends?

21 - Eagles may soar, but weasels don't get sucked into jet engines.

22 - What happens if you get scared half to death twice?

23 - My mechanic told me, "I couldn't repair your brakes, so I made your horn louder."

24 - Why do psychics have to ask you for your name?

25 - If at first you don't succeed, destroy all evidence that you tried.

26 - A conclusion is the place where you got tired of thinking.

27 - Experience is something you don't get until just after you need it.

28 - The hardness of the butter is proportional to the softness of the bread.

29 - To steal ideas from one person is plagiarism; to steal from many is research.

30 - The problem with the gene pool is that there is no lifeguard.

31 - The sooner you fall behind, the more time you'll have to catch up.

32 - The colder the X-ray table, the more of your body is required to be on it.

---

33 - Everyone has a photographic memory; some just don't have film.

34 - If your car could travel at the speed of light, would your headlights work?

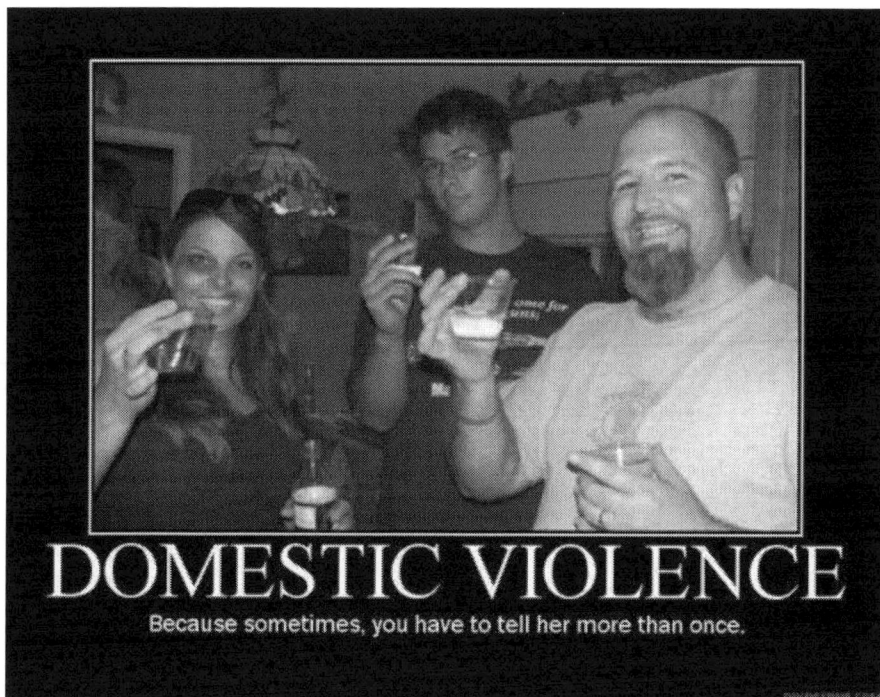

DOMESTIC VIOLENCE
Because sometimes, you have to tell her more than once.

Tools and their REAL uses:

DRILL PRESS: A tall upright machine useful for suddenly snatching flat metal bar stock out of your hands so that it smacks you in the chest and flings your beer across the room, splattering it against that freshly-stained heirloom piece you were drying.

WIRE WHEEL: Cleans paint off bolts and then throws them somewhere under the workbench with the speed of light. Also removes fingerprints and hard-earned guitar calluses from fingers in about the time it takes you to say, "Yeouw s--t..."

ELECTRIC HAND DRILL: Normally used for spinning pop rivets in their holes until you die of old age.

SKILL SAW: A portable cutting tool used to make studs too short.

PLIERS: Used to round off bolt heads. Sometimes used in the creation of blood-blisters. The most often the tool used by all women.

BELT SANDER: An electric sanding tool commonly used to convert minor touch-up jobs into major refinishing jobs.

HACKSAW: One of a family of cutting tools built on the Ouija board principle. It transforms human energy into a crooked, unpredictable motion, and the more you attempt to influence its course, the more dismal your future becomes.

VISE-GRIPS: Generally used after pliers to completely round off bolt heads. If nothing else is available, they can also be used to transfer intense welding heat to the palm of your hand.

WELDING GLOVES: Heavy duty leather gloves used to prolong the conduction of intense welding heat to the palm of your hand.

OXYACETYLENE TORCH: Used almost entirely for lighting various flammable objects in your shop on fire. Also handy for igniting the grease inside the wheel hub you want the bearing race out of.

WHITWORTH SOCKETS: Once used for working on older British cars and motorcycles, they are now used mainly for impersonating that 9/16 or ½ socket you've been searching for, over the last 45 minutes.

TABLE SAW: A large stationary power tool commonly used to launch wood projectiles for testing wall integrity.

HYDRAULIC FLOOR JACK: Used for lowering an automobile to the ground after you have installed your new brake shoes, trapping the jack handle firmly under the bumper.

EIGHT-FOOT LONG YELLOW PINE 4X4: Used for levering an automobile upward off of a trapped hydraulic jack handle.

TWEEZERS: A tool for removing wood splinters and so-sharp wire wheel wires.

E-Z OUT BOLT AND STUD EXTRACTOR: A tool ten times harder than any known drill bit that snaps neatly off in bolt holes thereby ending any possible future use.

RADIAL ARM SAW: A large stationary power saw primarily used by most shops to scare neophytes into choosing another line of work.

TWO-TON ENGINE HOIST: A tool for testing the maximum tensile strength of everything you forgot to disconnect.

CRAFTSMAN 1/2 x 24-INCH SCREWDRIVER: A very large pry bar that inexplicably has an accurately machined screwdriver tip on the end opposite the handle.

AVIATION METAL SNIPS: See hacksaw.

STRAIGHT SCREWDRIVER: A tool for opening paint cans. Sometimes used to convert common slotted screws into non-removable screws.

PRY BAR: A tool used to crumple the metal surrounding that clip or bracket you needed to remove in order to replace a 50 cent part.

TROUBLE LIGHT: The home mechanic's own tanning booth. Sometimes called a drop light, it is a good source of vitamin D,"the sunshine vitamin," which is not otherwise found under cars at night. Health benefits aside, its main purpose is to consume 40-watt light bulbs at about the same rate that 105mm howitzer shells might be used during, say, the first few hours of the Battle of the Bulge. More often dark than light, its name is somewhat misleading. The accessory socket within the base, has been permanently rendered useless, unless requiring a source of 117vac power to shock the mechanic senseless.

PHILLIPS SCREWDRIVER: Normally used to stab the vacuum seals under lids, opening old-style paper-and-tin oil cans and splashing oil on your shirt; but can also be used, as the name implies, to strip out Phillips screw heads. Women excel at using this tool.

AIR COMPRESSOR: A machine that takes energy produced in a coal-burning power plant 200 miles away and transforms it into compressed air that travels by hose to a Chicago Pneumatic impact wrench that grips rusty bolts which were last over tightened 30 years ago by someone at Ford, and instantly rounds off their heads. Also used to quickly snap off lug nuts.

HOSE CUTTER: A tool used to make hoses too short.

HAMMER: Originally employed as a weapon of war, the hammer nowadays is used as a kind of divining rod to locate the most expensive parts adjacent the object we are trying to hit. Women primarily use it to make gaping holes in walls when hanging pictures.

MECHANIC'S KNIFE: Used to open and slice through the contents of cardboard cartons delivered to your front door; works particularly well on contents such as seats, liquids in plastic bottles, collector magazines, refund checks, and rubber or plastic parts. Especially useful for slicing work clothes, but only while in use. It is also useful for removing large chunks of human flesh from the user's hands.

DAMNIT TOOL: Any handy tool that you grab and throw across the garage while yelling "DAMNIT" at the top of your lungs. It is also, most often, the next tool that you will need.

A Dirty Mind
If you got one you'll see it.

True or false: "This sentence is false."

Every Friday night after work, -sun, snow or rain - Jack, the Newfie, would fire up his outdoor grill and cook a moose steak. But, all of Jack's neighbors were Catholic. And since it was Lent, they were forbidden from eating meat on Friday. The delicious aroma from the grilled moose steaks was causing such a problem for the Catholic faithful that they finally talked to their priest. The priest came to visit Jack, and suggested that he become a Catholic. After several classes and much study, Jack attended Mass, and as the priest sprinkled holy water over him, he said: "You were born a Protestant and raised a Protestant, but now you are a Catholic." Jack's neighbors were greatly relieved, until Friday night arrived, and the wonderful aroma of grilled moose filled the neighborhood. The priest was called immediately by the neighbors, and, as he rushed into Jack's yard, clutching a rosary and prepared to scold him, he stopped and watched in amazement. There stood Jack, clutching a small bottle of holy water which he carefully sprinkled over the grilling meat and chanted: "You wuz born a moose, you wuz raised a moose, but now you is a Codfish."

My wife asked me, "How many women have you slept with? I proudly replied, "Only you, Darling. With all the others, I was awake."
The cast should be off by September.

There is a new study about women and how they feel about their asses; the results were pretty interesting: 30% of women think their ass is too fat… 10% of women think their ass is too skinny… The remaining 60% say they don't care, they love him, he's a good man and they wouldn't trade him for the world.

CLOWN FUNERAL

It's tragically hilarious

CHEERLEADER TRYOUTS

Hired.

A man and his wife are driving home one very cold night when the wife asks her husband to stop the car. There was a baby skunk lying at the side of the road, and she got out to see if it was still alive. It was, and she said to her husband, 'It's nearly frozen to death. Can we take it with us, get it warm, and let it go in the morning?' He says, 'OK, get in the car with it.' The wife says, 'Where shall I put it to get it warm?' He says, 'Put it between your legs. It's nice and warm there.' 'But what about the smell?' asked the wife. He says, 'Just hold its little nose.' The man is expected to recover, but the skunk she used to beat him died at the scene.

"YOU MAY BE A TALIBAN IF....."
1. You refine heroin for a living, but you have a moral objection to beer.
2. You own a $3,000 machine gun and a $5,000 rocket launcher, but you can't afford shoes.
3. You have more wives than teeth.
4. You wipe your butt with your bare left hand, but consider bacon "unclean".
5. You think vests come in two styles: bulletproof and suicide.
6. You can't think of anyone you haven't declared Jihad against.
7. You consider television dangerous, but routinely carry explosives in your clothing.
8. You were amazed to discover that cell phones have uses other than setting off bombs.
9. You have nothing against women and think every man should own at least one
10. You've always had a crush on your neighbor's goat.

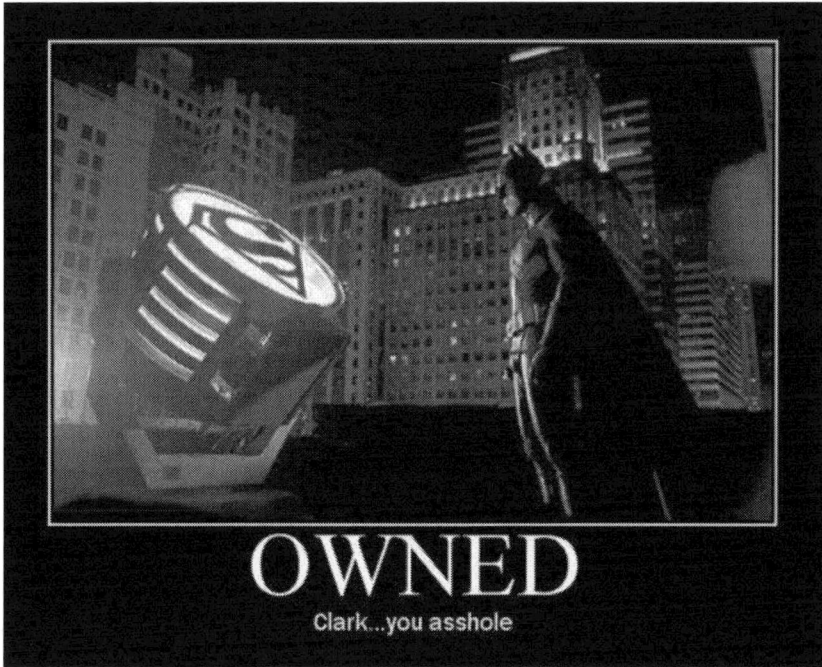

OWNED

Clark...you asshole

An old cowboy goes into a bar and orders a drink. As he sits there sipping whiskey, a young lady sits down next to him. She turns to the cowboy and asks him, "Are you a real cowboy?" He replies, "Well, I have spent my whole life on the ranch, herding horses, mending fences and branding cattle, so I guess I am." She says, " I'm a lesbian. I spend my whole day thinking about women. As soon as I get up in the morning I think about women. When I shower or watch TV, everything seems to make me think of women." A little while later a coupe sits down next to the old cowboy and asks him ,"Are you a real cowboy?" He replies, "I always thought I was, but I just found out I'm a lesbian."

AIM HIGH

What's the worst that could happen?

DIYDESPAIR.COM

I saw a fundamentalist Muslim extremist fall into the Rio Grande River this morning; he was struggling to stay afloat because of all the guns and bombs he was carrying. Along with him was an illegal Hispanic drug cartel member who was also struggling to stay afloat because of the large backpack of drugs that was strapped to his back.

If they didn't get help, they'd surely drown. Being a responsible Texan and abiding by the law to help those in distress, I informed the El Paso County Sheriff 's Office and Homeland Security. It is now 4pm, both have drowned, and neither authority has responded. I'm starting to think I wasted two stamps.

An old Italian Mafia Don is dying.. He calls his grandson to his bedside. "Elio, I wanna you lissina me. I wanna you to take-a my chrome plated .38 revolver so you will always remember me." "But grandpa, I really don't like guns. How about you leave me your Rolex watch instead?" "You lissina me, boy. Somma day you gonna be runna DA business, you gonna have a beautiful wife, lotsa money, a big-a home and maybe a couple of bambinos " "Somma day you gonna come-a home and maybe finda you wife inna bed with another man. "Whatta you gonna do then? Pointa to you watch and say, 'Time's Up'?"

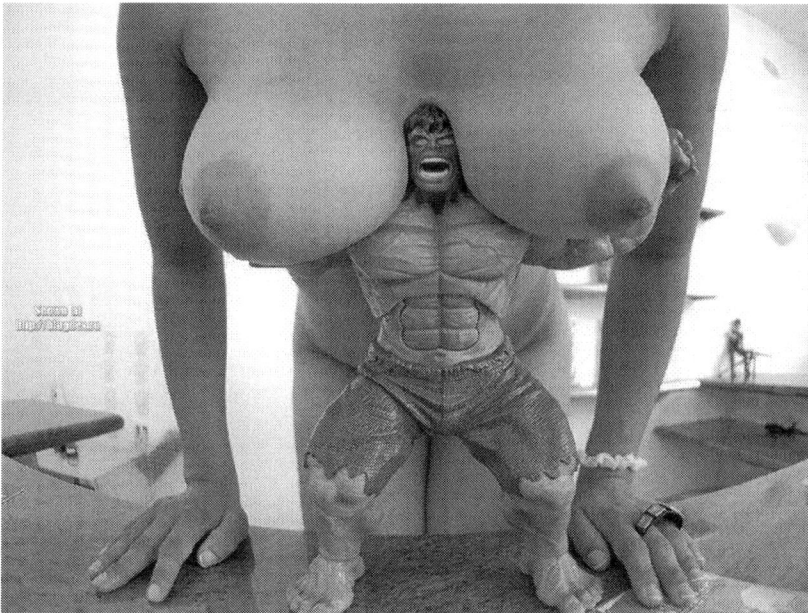

On some bases the Air Force is on one side of the field and civilian aircraft use the other side of the field, with the control tower in the middle. One day the tower received a call from an aircraft asking, "What time is it?"   The tower responded, "Who is calling?"   The aircraft replied, "What difference does it make?"   The tower replied, "It makes a lot of difference........If it is an Air Canada flight, it is 3 o'clock. If it is an Air Force plane, it is 1500 hours. If it is a Navy aircraft, it is 6 bells. If it is an Army aircraft, the big hand is on the 12 and the little hand is on the 3. If it is a Merchant Navy aircraft, it's Thursday afternoon and 120 minutes to "Happy Hour." ------- ----------------------- During training exercises, the lieutenant who was driving down a muddy back road encountered another car stuck in the mud with a red-faced colonel at the wheel. "Your jeep stuck, sir?" asked the lieutenant as he pulled alongside. "Nope," replied the colonel, coming over and handing him the keys, "yours is." ----------------------------- - Having just moved into his new office, a pompous new Commodore was sitting at his desk when a Navy rating knocked on the door. The Commodore quickly picked up the phone, told the Navy rating to enter, then said into the phone, "Yes, Admiral, I'll be seeing him this afternoon and I'll pass along your message. In the meantime, thank you for your good wishes, sir." Feeling as though he had sufficiently impressed the young enlisted man, he asked, "What do you want?" "Nothing important, sir," the Navy rating replied, "I'm just here to hook up your telephone." ------------------------ ------ Officer: "Sailor, do you have change for a dollar?" Sailor: "Sure, buddy." Officer: "That's no way to address an officer! Now let's try it again!" Officer: "Sailor. Do you have change for a dollar?" Soldier: "No, SIR!" ------------- ------------------ Q: How do you know if there is a fighter pilot at your party? A: He'll tell you. Q: What's the difference between God and fighter pilots? A: God doesn't think he's a fighter pilot.. Q: What's the difference between a fighter pilot and a jet engine? A: A jet engine stops whining when the plane shuts down. ------------------------------ An Air Force

Chief Master Sergeant and a General were sitting in the barbershop. They were both just getting finished with their shaves when the barbers reached for some after-shave to slap on their faces. The General shouted, "Hey, don't put that stuff on me! My wife will think I've been in a whorehouse!" The Chief turned to his barber and said, "Go ahead and put it on me. My wife doesn't know what the inside of a whorehouse smells like." ------------------------------- "Well," snarled the tough old Navy Chief to the bewildered Seaman, "I suppose after you get discharged from the Navy, you'll just be waiting for me to die so you can come and piss on my grave." "Not me, Chief!" the Seaman replied. "Once I get out of the Navy, I'm never going to stand in line again.

GIRL SCOUTS
Maybe next time you'll buy the fucking cookies

A stranger was seated next to a little girl on the airplane when the stranger turned to her and said, 'Let's talk. I've heard that flights go quicker if you strike up a conversation with your fellow passenger.' The little girl, who had just opened her book, closed it slowly and said to the stranger, 'What would you like to talk about?' 'Oh, I don't know,' said the stranger. 'How about nuclear power?' and he smiles. OK, ' she said 'That could be an interesting topic. But let me ask you a question first. A horse, a cow, and a deer all eat the same stuff - grass -. Yet a deer excretes little pellets, while a cow turns out a flat patty, and a horse produces clumps of dried grass. Why do you suppose that is?' The stranger, visibly surprised by the little girl's intelligence, thinks about it and says, 'Hmmm, I have no idea....' To which the little girl replies, 'Do you really feel qualified to discuss nuclear power when you don't know shit?

The Zen of Sarcasm
1. Do not walk behind me, for I may not lead. Do not walk ahead of me, for I may not follow. Do not walk beside me either. Just pretty much leave me alone.
2. The journey of a thousand miles begins with a broken fan belt and leaky tire.
3. It's always darkest before dawn. So if you're going to steal your neighbor's newspaper, that's the time to do it.
4. Don't be irreplaceable. If you can't be replaced, you can't be promoted.
5. Always remember that you're unique. Just like everyone else.
6. Never test the depth of the water with both feet.
7. If you think nobody cares if you're alive, try missing a couple of car payments.
8. Before you criticize someone, you should walk a mile in their shoes that way, when you criticize them, you're a mile away and you have their shoes.
9. If at first you don't succeed, skydiving is probably not for you.

10. Give a man a fish and he will eat for a day. Teach him how to fish, and he will sit in a boat and drink beer all day.

11.. If you lend someone $20 and never see that person again, it was probably a wise investment.

12 If you tell the truth, you don't have to remember anything.

13. Some days you're the bug; some days you're the windshield.

14. Everyone seems normal until you get to know them.

15. The quickest way to double your money is to fold it in half and put it back in your pocket.

16.. A closed mouth gathers no foot .

17. Duct tape is like 'The Force'. It has a light side and a dark side, and it holds the universe together.

18.. There are two theories to arguing with women. Neither one works.

19 .. Generally speaking, you aren't learning much when your lips are moving.

20. Experience is something you don't get until just after you need it

21 Never miss a good chance to shut up.

22 Never, under any circumstances, take a sleeping pill and a laxative on the same night.

Do they pay midgets under the table?

If you have seen one naked woman you want to see them all

Last Tuesday, as President Obama got off his Helicopter "Marine One" in front of the White House, he was carrying a baby Pig under each arm.

The squared away Marine guard snaps to attention, salutes and says: "Nice Pigs, sir."

The President replies "These are not mere Pigs Marine....these are authentic Arkansas Razorback Hogs!'

I got one for Secretary of State Hillary Clinton and I got the other one for Speaker of the House Nancy Pelosi.

"The squared away Marine again snaps to attention, salutes and says, "Excellent trade, sir."

A rubber stamp we all need..

If a Kingdom is run by a King, who runs a country?

Did You Know That the words race car spelled backward says
race car.   That eat is The only word that if you take the
1st letter and move it to the last, it spells it's past tense, ate.

And, Have you noticed that if you rearrange the letters in
"illegal immigrants," and add just a few more letters, it spells:
"Fuck off and go home you free-loading, benefit grabbing,
kid producing, violent, non-English speaking cocksuckers
and take those hairy faced, sandal wearing, bomb making,
goat fucking, smelly rag head bastards with you." How
weird is that?

Two tall trees, a birch and a beech, are growing in the woods. A small tree begins to grow between them, and the beech says to the birch, 'Is that a son of a beech or a son of a birch?' The birch says he cannot tell, but just then a woodpecker lands on the sapling.   The birch says, 'Woodpecker, you are a tree expert. Can you tell if that is a son of a beech or a son of a birch?'   The woodpecker takes a taste of the small tree and replies, 'It is neither a son of a beech nor a son of a birch. It is, however, the best little piece of ash I have ever poked my pecker into.'

THE MAGAZINE FOR MEN WHO DON'T MAKE THE DECISIONS

WHIPPED

Be your own boss
when she's not around

Coping with the loss of your friends
and the introduction of hers

Dealing with the absence of sex

10 new ways
to sleep on the couch

avoid confrontation
how to keep her happy
without getting yelled at

PLUS!
» Tips on lying
» How to get out of
her family events

MARCH 2003
$5.99 US £3.99

Please be very careful with E- Bay!!
PLEASE BE AWARE AND TAKE

NOTE OF E-BAY TRADERS,
 NOT SELLING AS ADVERTISED. I'VE
BEEN SCAMMED (bastards!)   I ORDERED A BLOW UP
DOLL.

AND THIS is what they sent...

I got a new set of wiper blades on my car (a Peugeot, made in France). I think they might be too big because they hang over the edges a little, but I don't care, they   work great and I would have to say that they are the only blades I have ever had that I actually like to watch working.

Call me crazy, but lately I have been driving around non-stop with them on. I've even been pulled over and the cop asked to go for a ride so he could watch them work.

 They were outrageously expensive (being French), but safety is my main concern and like I said, they work great. Let me know if you would like a pair for your car.

In the late 1700's, many houses consisted of a large room with only one chair. Commonly, a long wide board folded down from the wall, and was used for dining. The 'head of the household' always sat in the chair while everyone else ate sitting on the floor. Occasionally a guest, who was usually a man, would be invited to sit in this chair during a meal. To sit in the chair meant you were important and in charge. They called the one sitting in the chair the 'chair man.' Today in business, we use the expression or title 'Chairman' or 'Chairman of the Board.'

It's people!
Spam is made
of people!

dribbleglass.com

A man in the Safeway Store tries to buy half a head of lettuce. The very young produce assistant tells him that they sell only whole heads of lettuce. The man persists and asks to see the manager. The boy says he'll ask his manager about it walking into the back room, the boy said to his manager, "Some ass hole wants to buy half a head of lettuce." As he finished his sentence, he turned to find the man standing right behind him, so he added, "And this gentleman has kindly offered to buy the other half" The manager approved the deal, and the man went on his way. Later the manager said to the boy, "I was impressed with the way you got yourself out of that situation earlier. We like people who think on their feet here Where are you from, son?"" Canada, sir," the boy replied.'Well, why did you leave Canada?" the manager asked. The boy said, "Sir, there's nothing but whores and hockey players up there."Really?" said the manager. "My wife is from Canada." No shit?" replied the boy. "Who'd she play for?"

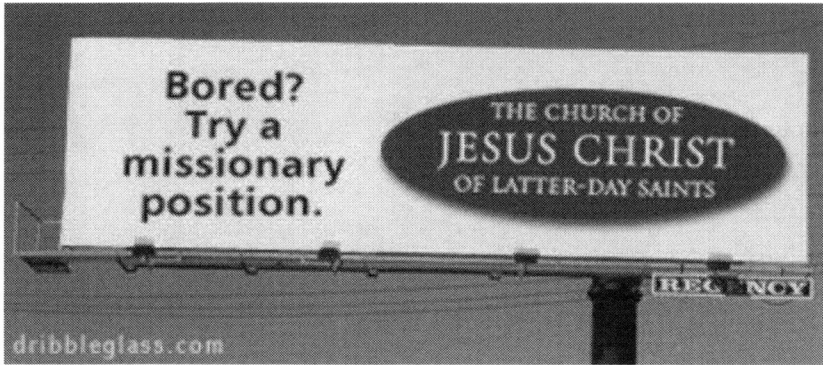

An older gentleman had an appointment to see the urologist who shared offices with several other doctors. The waiting room was filled with patients. As he approached the receptionist's desk, he noticed that the receptionist was a large unfriendly woman who looked like a Sumo wrestler. He gave her his name. In a very loud voice, the receptionist said, "YES, I HAVE YOUR NAME HERE; YOU WANT TO SEE THE DOCTOR ABOUT IMPOTENCE, RIGHT?" All the patients in the waiting room snapped their heads around to look at the very embarrassed man. He recovered quickly, and in an equally loud voice replied,'NO, I'VE COME TO INQUIRE ABOUT A SEX CHANGE OPERATION, BUT I DON'T WANT THE SAME DOCTOR THAT DID YOURS.'

Paddy is passing by Mick's hay shed one day when through a gap in the door he sees Mick doing a slow and sensual striptease in front of an old red Massey Ferguson. Buttocks clenched he performs a slow pirouette and gently slides off first the right welly, followed by the left. He then hunches his shoulders forward and in a classic striptease move lets his braces fall down from his shoulders to dangle by his hips over his corduroy trousers.

Grabbing both sides of his check shirt he rips it apart to reveal his tea stained vest underneath and with a final flourish he hurls his flat cap on to a pile of hay.' What on earth are you doing Mick' says Paddy 'Jeez Paddy, ye frightened the livin bejasus out of me' says an obviously embarrassed Mick, 'but me and the Missus been having some trouble lately in the bedroom department, and the Therapist suggested I do something sexy to a tractor. "

Screw it. Nothing else is open at this hour. **Denny's**

We're proud of our privates. **U.S. ARMY**

So much easier than parenting. RITALIN

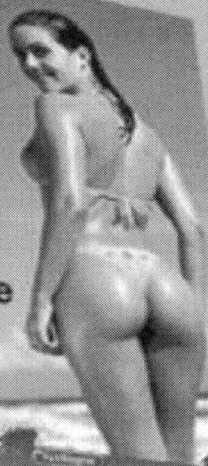

Like her mugs? You should see her cans.

ST. PAULI GIRL

dribbleglass.com

The kids filed back into class Monday morning. They were very excited. Their weekend assignment was to sell something, then give a talk on productive salesmanship.

Little Sally led off: "I sold girl scout cookies and I made $30," she said proudly, "My sales approach was to appeal to the customer's civil spirit and I credit that approach for my obvious success." "Very good," said the teacher. Little Jenny was next: "I sold magazines," she said, "I made $45 and I explained to everyone that magazines would keep them up on current events." "Very good, Jenny," said the teacher.
    Eventually, it was little Johnny's turn (you remember him don't cha?). The teacher held her breath ... Little Johnny walked to the front of the classroom and dumped a box full of cash on the teacher's desk. "$2,467," he said. "$2,467!" cried the teacher, "What in the world were you selling?"

270

"Toothbrushes," said little Johnny.   "Toothbrushes!" echoed the teacher, "How could you possibly sell enough tooth brushes to make that much money?"   "I found the busiest corner in town," said little Johnny, "I set up a Dip & Chip stand and gave everybody who walked by a free sample."

They all said the same thing, "Hey, this tastes like dog shit!"

Then I would say, "It is dog shit. Wanna buy a toothbrush?"

"I used the governmental approach of giving you something shitty for free, and then making you pay to get the shitty taste out of your mouth."

dribbleglass.com
GOLD'S GYM
Big egos.
Big biceps.
Little winkies.

dribbleglass.com
Making us all wish
we were blind.
SPEEDO

dribbleglass.com
ELLER
Come check out
our stool
samples.
IKEA

Two businessmen in Florida were sitting down for a break in their "soon-to-be" new store. As yet, the store wasn't ready, with only a few shelves set up. One said to the other, "I bet any minute now some senior is going to walk by, put his face to the window, and ask what we're selling." No sooner were the words out of his mouth when, sure enough, a curious senior walked to the window, had a peek, and in a soft voice asked, "What are you sellin' here?" One of the men replied sarcastically, "We're selling ass-holes." Without skipping a beat the old timer said, "Must be doing well...Only two left."

dribbleglass.com

If drinking and driving is illegal, then why do bars have parking lots?

Two nuns driving down the road. A Vampire jumps down onto the hood of their car.

"Quick"! Says one nun, "Show him your cross".

The other nun leans out the window and yells, "Get off the fucking car!

A frustrated wife buys a pair of crotchless panties in an attempt to spice up her dead sex-life. She puts them on, together with a short skirt and sits on the sofa opposite her husband. At strategic moments she uncrosses her legs ... enough times till her husband says... "Are you wearing crotch less panties?" "Y-e-s," she answers with a seductive smile. "Thank God for that... I thought you were sitting on the cat. He never heard the gunshot.

Men socialize by insulting each other, but don't really mean it.

Women socialize by complimenting each other, but don't really mean it.

JAILBAIT

They Call This Entrapment.

My wife sat down on the couch next to me as I was flipping channels. She asked, 'What's on TV?' I said, 'Dust.' And that's when the fight started .... My wife and I were watching Who Wants To Be A Millionaire while we were in bed. I turned to her and said, "Do you want to have sex?" "No," she answered. I then said, "Is that your final answer?" She didn't even look at me this time, simply saying "Yes.." So I said, "Then I'd like to phone a friend." And that's when the fight started ... .
I asked my wife, "Where do you want to go for our anniversary?" It warmed my heart to see her face melt in sweet appreciation. "Somewhere I haven't been in a long time!" she said.. So I suggested, "How about the kitchen?" And that's when the fight started... ....

Saturday morning I got up early, quietly dressed, made my lunch, grabbed the dog, and slipped quietly into the garage... I hooked up the boat up to the truck, and proceeded to back out into a torrential downpour. The wind was blowing 50 mph, so I pulled back into the garage, turned on the radio, and discovered that the weather would be bad all day. I went back into the house, quietly undressed, and slipped back into bed. I cuddled up to my wife's back, now with a different anticipation, and whispered, 'The weather out there is terrible.' My loving wife of 10 years replied, 'Can you believe my stupid husband is out fishing in that?' And that's when the fight started... .... A man and a woman were asleep like two innocent babies. Suddenly, at 3 o'clock in the morning, a loud noise came from outside. The woman, bewildered, jumped up from the bed and yelled at the man 'Holy Crap. That must be my husband!' So the man jumped out of the bed; scared and naked jumped out the window. He smashed himself on the ground, ran through a thorn bush and to his car as fast as he could go. A few minutes later he returned and went up to the bedroom and screamed at the woman, 'I AM your husband!' The woman yelled back, 'Yeah, then why were you running?' And that's when the fight started.... .... I tried to talk my wife into buying a case of Molson Canadian for $24.95. Instead, she bought a jar of face cream for $17.95. I told her the beer would make her look better at night than the face cream And that's when the fight started..... .... A woman was standing nude, looking in the bedroom mirror. She was not happy with what she saw and said to her husband, 'I feel horrible; I look old, fat and ugly. I really need you to pay me a compliment.' The husband replies, 'Your eyesight's damn near perfect.' And that's when the fight started.... .... I took my wife to a restaurant. The waiter, for some reason, took my order first. "I'll have the strip steak, medium rare, please." He said, "Aren't you worried about the mad cow?"" Nah, she can order for herself..." And that's when the fight started.... .... My wife and I were sitting at a table at my high school reunion, and I kept staring at a drunken lady swigging her drink as she sat alone at a nearby table. My wife asked, 'Do you know her?' 'Yes,' I sighed, 'She's my old girlfriend. I understand she took to drinking right after we split up those many years ago, and I hear she hasn't been sober since.' 'My God!' said my wife, 'who would think a person could go on celebrating that long?' And that's when the fight started.... .... After retiring, I went to the Social Security office to apply for my SIN The woman behind the counter asked me for my driver's license to verify my age. I looked in my pockets and realized I had left my wallet at home. I told the woman that I was very sorry, but I would have to go home and come back later. The woman said, 'Unbutton your shirt.' So I opened my shirt revealing my curly silver hair. She said, 'That silver hair on your chest is proof enough for me' and she processed my Social Security application. When I got home, I excitedly told my wife about my experience at the Social Security office. She said, 'You should have dropped your pants. You might have gotten disability, too.' And that's when the fight started.. When I got home last night, my wife demanded that I take her someplace expensive... so, I took her to a gas station. And that's when the fight started.. My wife was hinting about what she wanted for our upcoming anniversary. She said, 'I want something shiny that goes from 0 to 150 in about 3 seconds. I bought her a bathroom scale. And that's when the fight started....................................... One year, a husband decided to buy his mother-in-law a cemetery plot as a Christmas gift. The next year, he didn't buy her a gift. When she asked him why, he replied, "Well, you still haven't used the gift I bought you last year!" And that's when the fight started....

JUST GOOD FRIENDS
Real Good Friends

A bear walks into a bar. The waitress says "we don't serve bears". The bear eats the waitress. The bar tender says we don't serve anyone who uses drugs. "What drugs?" the bear asks. "What about the bar bitch you ate?"

With enough thrust, pigs fly just fine.

TEAMWORK

Because bullets can only go through so many bodies.

A young cowboy from Montana goes off to college. Halfway through the semester, he has foolishly squandered all his money. Trying desperately to think of a way to get his father to send more money, he remembers how much his dad loves his old hound dog, Ol' Blue..He calls home. "Dad," he says, "You won't believe what modern education is developing! They actually have a program here in Missoula that will teach your dog, Ol' Blue, how to talk!" "That's amazing," his Dad says. "How do I get Ol' Blue in that program?" "Just send him down here with $1,000" the young cowboy says. "I'll get him in the course." So, his father sends the dog and $1,000. About two-thirds of the way through the semester, the money again runs out. The boy calls home. "So how's Ol' Blue doing son?" his father asks."Awesome, Dad, he's talking up a storm," he says, "but you just won't believe this - they've had such good results they have started to teach the animals how to read!"

"Read!?" says his father, "No kidding! How do we get Blue into that program?" "Just send $2,500, I'll get him in the class." The money promptly arrives. But our hero has a problem. It's the end of the school year, and his father will find out the dog can neither talk, nor read. So he shoots the dog.When he arrives home at the end of the year, his father is all excited. "Where's Ol' Blue? I just can't wait to see him read something and talk!" "Dad," the boy says, "I have some grim news. Yesterday morning, just before we left to drive home, Ol' Blue was in the living room, kicked back in the recliner, reading the Wall Street Journal, like he usually does. Then he turned to me and asked, "So, is your daddy still messing around with that little redhead who lives down the street?" The father exclaimed, "I hope you shot that sumbitch before he talks to your Mother!" "I sure did, Dad!" "That's my boy!" The kid went on to become a successful lawyer and then went into politics.

The Newfie fisherman went to the hospital as his wife was having a baby. Upon arriving the nurse explains, "It was a difficult delivery. Your wife has had quints, 5 big baby boys." Newfie says proudly, "I'm not surprised, I have a penis on me like a chimney!"
The nurse replies, "You might want to consider getting it cleaned, the babies are all black."

A tough looking biker was riding his Harley when he sees a girl about to jump off a bridge so he stops.
"What are you doing?" he asks "I'm going to commit suicide," she says. While he did not want to appear insensitive, he didn't want to miss an opportunity, so he asks "Well, before you jump, why don't you give me a Kiss?" So, she does. After she's finished, the biker says, "Wow! That was the best kiss I have ever had. That's a real talent you are wasting. You could be famous. Why are you committing suicide?"
"My parents don't like me dressing up like a girl......"

HOUSE FOR SALE
BY OWNER
BECAUSE
MY NEIGHBOR'S AN
ASSHOLE!

HONESTY

A Rare Commodity In Real Estate Advertising

Beer contains female hormones! Yes, that's right, FEMALE hormones!

Last month, Montreal University and scientists released the results of a recent analysis that revealed the presence of female hormones in beer. Men should take a concerned look at their beer consumption. The theory is that beer contains female hormones (hops contain Phytoestrogens) and that by drinking enough beer, men turn into women. To test the theory, 100 men each drank 8 schooners of beer within a one (1) hour period. It was then observed that 100% of the test subjects, yes, 100% of all these men:-

1) Argued over nothing.

2) Refused to apologize when obviously wrong.

3) Gained weight.

4) Talked excessively without making sense.

5) Became overly emotional

6) Couldn't drive.

7) Failed to think rationally, and

8) Had to sit down while urinating.   No further testing was considered necessary!!

After Monday and Tuesday even the calendar says WTF.

Wine improves with age. I improve with wine.

Without music life would **B**♭

A man owned a small farm in North Dakota. The North Dakota Dept of Fair Labor Practices claimed he was not paying proper wages to his help and sent an agent out to interview him. "I need a list of your employees and how much you pay them, demanded the Agent." "Well," replied the farmer, "there's my farm hand who's been with me 3 years. I pay him $400 a week plus free room and board. The cook has been here for 18 months and I pay her $300 per week plus free room and board. There's the half-wit. He works about 18 hours a day and does about 90% of all the work around here. He makes about $10 per week, pays his own room and board, and I buy him a bottle of Bourbon every Saturday night. He also sleeps with my wife occasionally." "That's the guy I want to talk to....the half-wit," says the Agent.
"That would be me", replied the farmer.

YOU ARE BEING MONITORED

The wife and I were sitting around the breakfast table one lazy Sunday morning.
I said to her, "If I were to die suddenly, I want you to immediately sell all my stuff."

"Now why would you want me to do something like that?" she asked.

"I figure that you would eventually remarry and I don't want some other asshole using my stuff."

She looked at me and said: "What makes you think I'd marry another asshole?"

Larry and Mel are quietly sitting in a boat fishing, chewing tobacco, and drinking beer when suddenly Mel says," Think I'm gonna divorce the wife. She ain't spoke to me in over two months."

Larry spits overboard, takes a long, slow sip of beer, and says, "Better think it over. Women like that are hard to find."

Top Ten Country Western Songs.

10. I Hate Every Bone In Her Body But Mine
 9. I Ain't Never Gone To Bed With an Ugly Woman But I Woke Up With A Few
 8. If The Phone Don't Ring, You'll Know It's Me
 7. I've Missed You, But My Aim's Improvin'
 6. Wouldn't Take Her To A Dogfight 'Cause I'm Scared She'd Win

5. I'm So Miserable Without You It's Like You're Still Here
4. My Wife Ran Off With My Best Friend And I Miss Him
3.. She Took My Ring and Gave Me the Finger
2. She's Lookin' Better with Every Beer

And the Number One Country & Western song is...
 1. It's Hard To Kiss The Lips At Night That Chewed My Ass All Day

A hooded robber burst into a Texas bank and forced the tellers to load a sack full of cash.
On his way out the door, a brave Texas customer grabbed the hood and pulled it off revealing the robber's face. The robber shot the customer without a moment's hesitation. He then looked around the bank and noticed one of the tellers looking straight at him. The robber instantly shot him also. Everyone else, by now very scared, looked intently down at the floor in silence. The robber yelled, 'Well, did anyone else see my face?' There are a few moments of utter silence in which everyone was plainly afraid to speak. Then, one old cowboy tentatively raised his hand, and while keeping his head down said, 'My wife got a pretty good look at you.'

My wife and I were at home watching TV. I had the remote and was switching back and forth between a fishing channel and the porn channel. She became more and more annoyed and finally said: For God's sakes, leave it on the porn channel. You already know how to fish.

Two wrongs don't make a right but three rights make a left.

Earth without art is just eh.

If life gives you melons you might be dyslexic.

Back in my day we had nine planets.

1. Coffee (n.), the person upon whom one coughs.

_____

2. Flabbergasted (adj.), appalled over how much weight you have gained.

3. Abdicate (v.), to give up all hope of ever having a flat stomach.

4. Esplanade (v.), to attempt an explanation while drunk.

5. Willy-nilly (adj.), impotent.

6. Negligent (adj.), a condition in which you absentmindedly answer the door in your nightgown.

7. Lymph (v.), to walk with a lisp.

8. Gargoyle (n), olive-flavoured mouthwash.

9. Flatulence (n.) emergency vehicle that picks you up after you are run over by a steamroller.

10. Balderdash (n.), a rapidly receding hairline.

11. Testicle (n.), a humorous question on an exam.

12. Rectitude (n.), the formal, dignified bearing adopted by proctologists.

13. Pokemon (n), Rastafarian proctologist.

14. Oyster (n.), person who sprinkles his conversation with Yiddishisms.

15. Frisbeetarianism (n.), (back by popular demand): The belief that, when you die, your soul flies up onto the roof and gets stuck there.

16. Circumvent (n.), opening in the front of boxer shorts worn by Jewish men.

The Washington Post's Style Invitational also asked readers to take any word from the dictionary, alter it by adding, subtracting, or changing one letter, and supply a new definition. **Here are this year's winners:**

1. Bozone (n.): The substance surrounding stupid people that stops bright ideas from penetrating. The bozone layer, unfortunately, shows little sign of breaking down in the near future.

2. Foreploy (v): Any misrepresentation about yourself for the purpose of getting laid.

3. Cashtration (n.): The act of buying a house, which renders the subject financially impotent for an indefinite period.

4. Giraffiti (n): Vandalism spray-painted very, very high.
5. Sarchasm (n): The gulf between the author of sarcastic wit and the person who doesn't get it.
6. Inoculatte (v): To take coffee intravenously when you are running late.
7. Hipatitis (n): Terminal coolness.
8. Osteopornosis (n): A degenerate disease. (that one got extra credit)
9. Karmageddon (n): Its like, when everybody is sending off all these really bad vibes, right? And then, like, the Earth explodes and it's like, a serious bummer.
10. Decafalon (n.): The grueling event of getting through the day consuming only things that are good for you.
11. Glibido (v): All talk and no action.
12. Dopeler effect (n): The tendency of stupid ideas to seem smarter when they come at you rapidly.
13. Arachnoleptic fit (n.): The frantic dance performed just after you've accidentally walked through a spider web.
14. Beelzebug (n.): Satan in the form of a mosquito that gets into your bedroom at three in the morning and cannot be cast out.
15. Caterpallor (n.): The colour you turn after finding half a grub in the fruit you're eating
16. Ignoranus (n): A person who's both stupid and an asshole.

FUCK THIS SHIT
I'll be a stripper

At the end of the tax year, Revenue Canada office sent an inspector to audit the books of a local hospital. While the auditor was checking the books he turned to the CFO of the hospital and said, "I notice you buy a lot of bandages. What do you do with the end of the roll when there's too little left to be of any use?"

"Good question," noted the CFO. "We save them up and send them back to the bandage company, and every now and then they send us a free box of bandages."

"Oh," replied the auditor, somewhat disappointed that his unusual question had a practical answer. But on he went, in his obnoxious way.

"What about all these plaster purchases? What do you do with what's left over after setting a cast on a patient?"

"Ah, yes," replied the CFO, realizing that the inspector was trying to trap him with an unanswerable question. "We save it and send it back to the manufacturer, and every now and then they send us a free package of plaster."

"I see," replied the auditor, thinking hard about how he could fluster the know-it-all CFO.

"Well," he went on, "What do you do with all the leftover foreskins from the circumcisions you perform?"
"Here, too, we do not waste," answered the CFO. "What we do is save all the little foreskins and send them to Revenue Canada, and about once a year they send us a complete dick."

A man was sitting on a blanket at the beach. He had no arms and no legs. Three women, from England, Wales, and Scotland, were walking past and felt sorry for the poor man.
The English woman said "Have you ever had a hug?"
The man said "No," so she gave him a hug and walked on.
The Welsh woman said, "Have you ever had a kiss?"
The man said, "No," so she gave him a kiss and walked on.
The Scottish woman came to him and said, "'Ave ya ever been fooked, laddie?"
The man broke into a big smile and said, "No".
She said, "Aye, ya will be when the tide comes in."

A guy is out with his buddies. He has a few drinks, gets in the mood but true to his wife goes home. When he gets home he finds her sound asleep in bed with her mouth wide open.
He gets two aspirin and drops them into her mouth.
Of course, she chokes but recovers and asks, "What did you put in my mouth??" He says, "Two aspirin".
She replies, "BUT I DON'T HAVE A HEADACHE"!!!
He says, "That's what I wanted to hear."

One of the questions from the career placement test given college student applicants for a military commission.
"Rearrange the letters P N E S I to spell out an important part of human body that is more useful when erect!"
Those who answered "spine" went to medical school...the rest went to pilot training.

Dear God,

———

292

My prayer for this year is for a fat bank account & a thin body. Please don't mix these up like you did last year. Amen!

It 's not whether you win or lose, but how you place the blame.

You are not drunk if you can lie on the floor without holding on.

We have enough youth. How about a fountain of "smart"?

The original point and click interface was a Smith & Wesson.

A fool and his money can throw one heck of a party.

When blondes have more fun do they know it?

Five days a week my body is a temple. The other two it's an amusement park

Money isn't everything, but it sure keeps the kids in touch.

CLOWN BOMB

When you see it, you will laugh, then feel very terrible.

Don't Drink and Drive. You might hit a bump and spill something.

If at first you don't succeed, skydiving is not for you.

Reality is only an illusion that occurs due to a lack of alcohol.

Time's fun when you're having flies. ...*Kermit the Frog*

We are born naked, wet and hungry. Then things get worse.

Red meat is not bad for you. Fuzzy green meat is bad for you.

Ninety-nine percent of all lawyers give the rest a bad name.

One good thing about Alzheimer's is you get to meet new people every day.

Xerox and Wurlitzer will merge to produce reproductive organs.

Alabama state motto: At least we're not Mississippi.

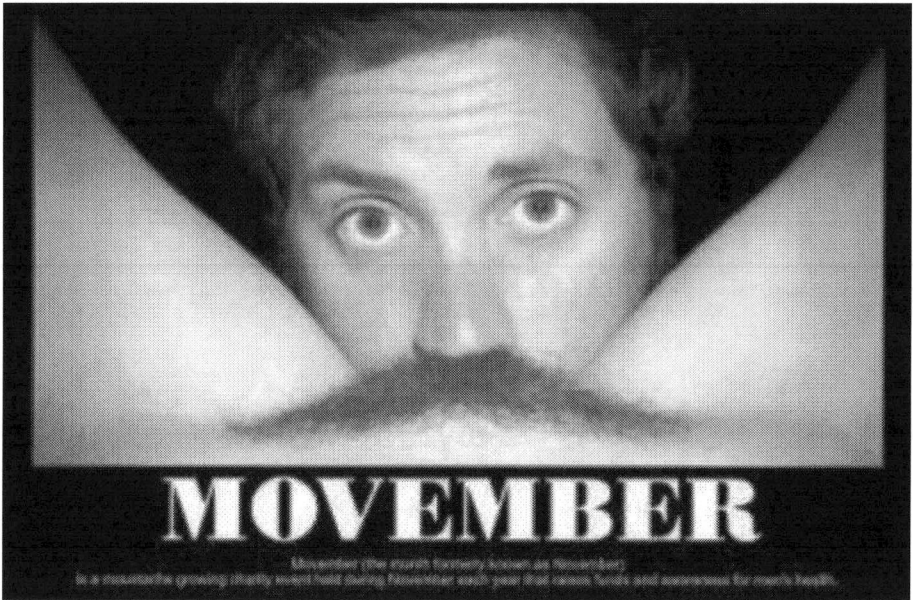

MOVEMBER

The latest survey shows that three out of four people make up 75% of the population.

You know why a banana is like a politician? When he first comes in he is green, then he turns yellow and then he's rotten.

I think Congressmen should wear uniforms like NASCAR drivers so we could identify their corporate sponsors.

Silent and listen use the same letters.

Be yourself - everyone else is taken.

I am so busy I don't know if I found a rope or lost a horse.

VERY STRANGE..... Did You Know That the words race car spelled backward says race car. That eat is the only word that if you take the 1st letter and move it to the last, it spells it's past tense, ate. And, have you noticed that if you rearrange the letters in "illegal immigrants," and add just a few more letters, it spells: "Fuck off and go home you free-loading, benefit grabbing, kid producing, violent, non-English speaking cocksuckers and take those hairy faced, sandal wearing, bomb making, goat fucking, smelly rag head bastards with you." How weird is that?

The female dentist pulls out a numbing needle to give the man a shot of Novocain.

"No way! No needles. I hate needles" the patient said..

The dentist starts to hook up the nitrous oxide and the man

objects.

"I can't do the gas thing. The thought of having the gas mask on, suffocates me!"

The dentist then asks the patient if he has any objection to taking a pill.

"No objection," the patient says. "'I'm fine with pills."

The dentist then returns and says, "Here's a Viagra."

The patient says, "Wow! I didn't know Viagra worked as a pain killer!"

"It doesn't", said the dentist, "but it's going to give you something to hold on to when I pull your tooth.

I vote **Republican** to keep Foreigners, Minorities, Women, Socialist, Gays, and Liberals from **ruining** my life.

I vote **Republican** to keep this moron from realizing I'm the only one **ruining** his life.

An elderly man is stopped by the police around 2 a.m. and is asked where he is going at this time of night.

The man replies, "I am on my way to a lecture about alcohol abuse and the effects it has on the human body, as well as smoking and staying out late.

"The officer then asks, "Really? Who's giving that lecture at this time of night?" The man replies,

"That would be my wife."

Spinning Jenny discovered steam at the Battle of Cardigan.

A first-grade teacher, Ms Brooks, was having trouble with one of her students. The teacher asked, "Harry, what's your problem?"
Harry answered, "I'm too smart for the 1st grade. My sister is in the 3rd grade and I'm smarter than she is! I think I should be in the 3rd grade too!"
Ms. Brooks had enough. She took Harry to the principal's office.
While Harry waited in the outer office, the teacher explained to the principal what the situation was. The principal told Ms. Brooks he would give the boy a test. If he failed to answer any of his questions he was to go back to the 1st grade and behave. She agreed.
Harry was brought in and the conditions were explained to him and he agreed to take the test.
Principal: "What is 3 x 3?"
Harry: "9."
Principal: "What is 6 x 6?"
Harry: "36."
And so it went with every question the principal thought a 3rd grader should know.
The principal looks at Ms. Brooks and tells her, "I think Harry can go to the 3rd grade."

Ms. Brooks says to the principal, "Let me ask him some questions."

The principal and Harry both agreed.

Ms. Brooks asks, "What does a cow have four of that I have only two of?"

Harry, after a moment: "Legs."

Ms Brooks: "What is in your pants that you have but I do not have?"

The principal wondered why would she ask such a question! Harry replied: "Pockets."

Ms. Brooks: "What does a dog do that a man steps into?"

Harry: "Pants."

The principal sat forward with his mouth hanging open.

Ms. Brooks: "What goes in hard and pink then comes out soft and sticky?"

The principal's eyes opened really wide and before he could stop the answer, Harry replied, "Bubble gum."

Ms. Brooks: "What does a man do standing up, a woman does sitting down and a dog does on three legs?"

Harry: "Shake hands."

The principal was trembling.

Ms. Brooks: "What word starts with an 'F' and ends in 'K' that means a lot of heat and excitement?"

Harry: "Firetruck."

The principal breathed a sigh of relief and told the teacher, "Put Harry in the fifth-grade, I got the last six questions wrong... "

What is blue and smells like red paint? Blue paint.

Why did the boy drop his ice cream? Because he was hit by a bus.

What's worse than finding a worm in your apple? The Holocaust.

A dyslexic man walks into a bra.

300

How do you confuse a blonde? Paint yourself green and throw forks at her.

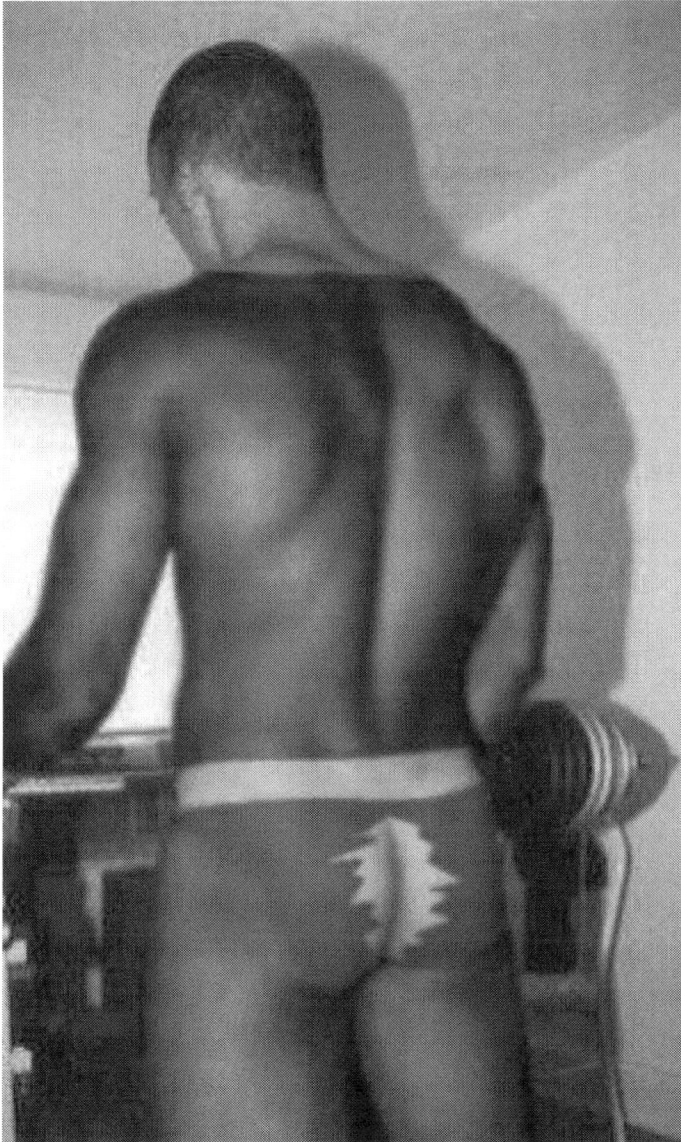

When a woman wears too much make - up

A farmer tells the new groom "Enjoy it. When you are first married it is like a nice little bird's nest but after 40 years and 6 kids it is like a cow pie with a wagon rut through it."

Little Billy shows Little Sally his new shoes. She has better ones. He shows her his new bike. She has a better one. He shows her his penis. She shows him her pussy and says, "With one of these, I can have as many of those as I want."

www.verparacreer.net

A grasshopper walks into a bar. The bartender says "Hey we have a drink named after you." "Really?" the grasshopper replies, " You have a drink named Steve?"

What does oral sex in a retirement home taste like? Depends.

Why did God invent Gentiles? Someone has to pay retail.

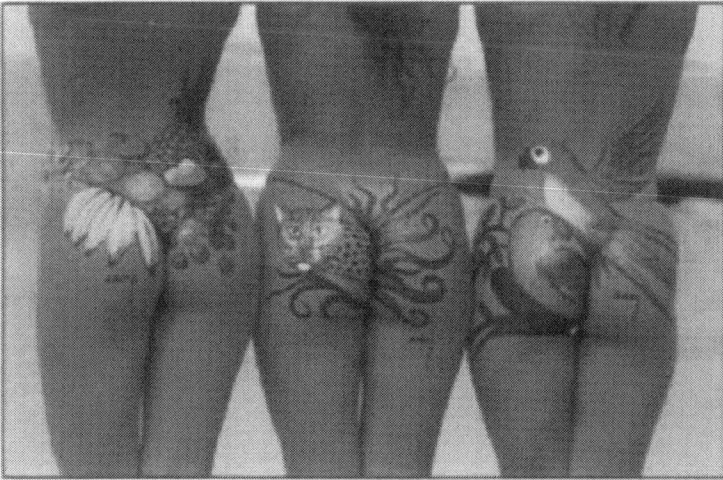

This is a frightening statistic.
25% of women in this country are on medication for mental illness.
That's bloody scary......
It means 75% are running around with no medication at all!

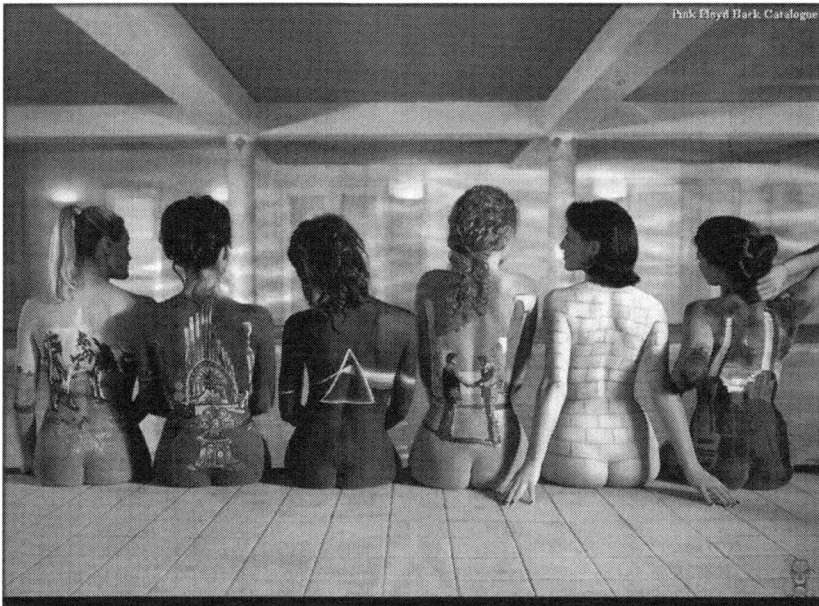

Bernadette Taylor © 1994

What did one saggy boob say to the other saggy boob? "We'd better perk up or people will think we are nuts."

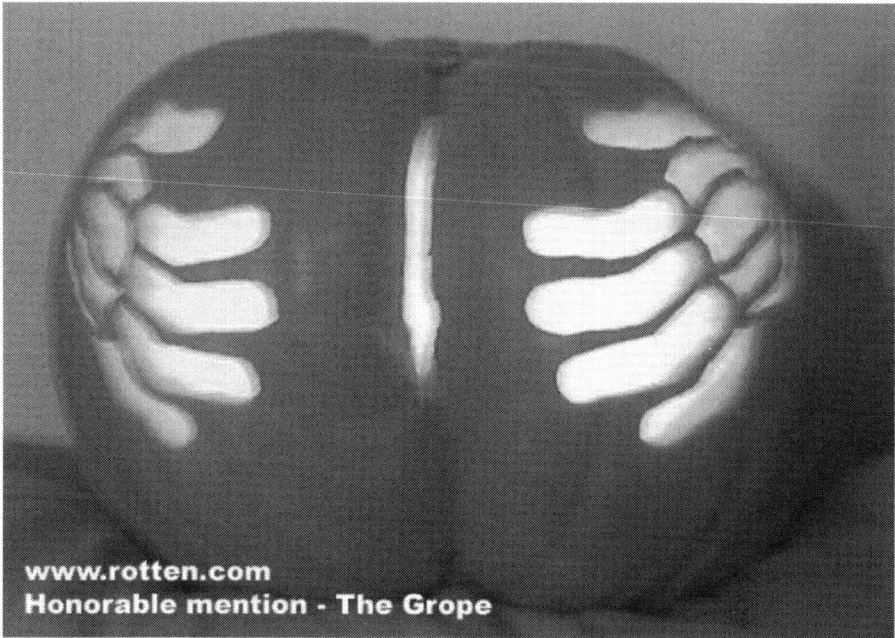

An old Cherokee told his grandson: "My son, there's a battle between two wolves inside us all. One is Evil. It's anger, jealousy, greed, resentment, inferiority, lies and ego. The other is Good. It's joy, peace, love, hope, humility, kindness and truth." The boy thought about it and asked: "Grandfather, which wolf wins?". The old man quietly replied: "The one you feed."

Did you hear about the guy whose whole left side was cut off? He's all right now.

I'm reading a book about anti-gravity. It's impossible to put down.

It's not that the man did not know how to juggle, he just didn't have the balls to do it.

www.verparacreer.com

There was a sign on the lawn at a drug re-hab center that said 'Keep off the Grass'.

I used to have a fear of hurdles, but I got over it.

Einstein developed a theory about space, and it was about time too.

Atheism is a non-prophet organization.

Show me a piano falling down a mineshaft and I'll show you A-flat minor.

To write with a broken pencil is pointless.

How do you recognize an outgoing engineer? He looks at your shoes when talking to you

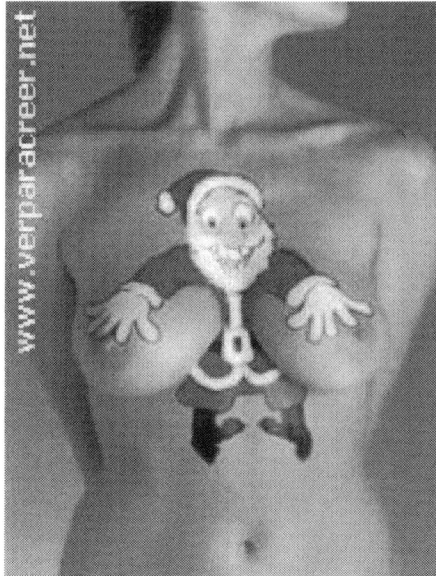

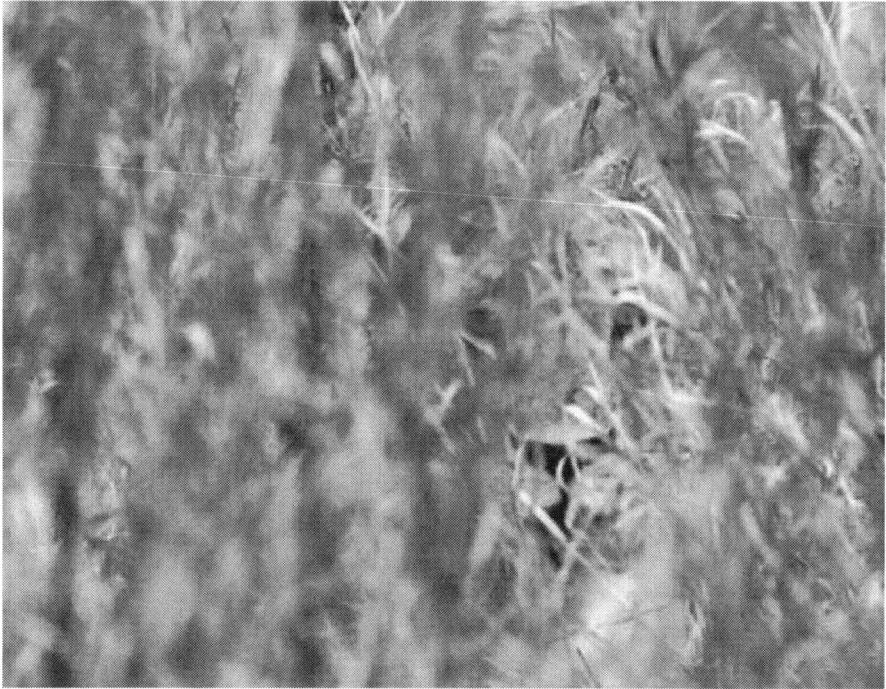

LEGO GUMMIES

WHEN YOU EAT THEM, YOU WILL SHIT BRICKS

Everytime I see a math word problem it looks like this:
If I have 10 ice cubes and you have 11 apples.
How many pancakes will fit on the roof?
Answer:
Purple because aliens
don't wear hats.

arrg! ecards

I got yer stimulus package right here.

.com BLUNTCARD

The latest survey shows that three out of four people make up 75% of the population.

I was in the pet shop last week when I noticed a Muslim with the most amazingly colored parrot perched on his shoulder...
"Where did you get that from?" I asked,
 "Toronto, there's fucking thousands of them!" said the Parrot.

Blonde Phone Call
"Hi Mom, How are you?"
"Hi Sally, where are you? I thought you were with your father at the Ace Hardware"
"Yeah we were, but I got arrested, and they've let me make one phone call"
"What happened?"
"Oh, I punched this African-American woman in the head."
"What on earth, why did you do that?"
"Well it wasn't my fault. Dad told me to find a Black & Decker."

Students in an advanced Biology class were taking their mid-term exam. The last question was, 'Name seven advantages of Mother's Milk.' The question was worth 70 points or none at all. One student, in particular, was hard put to think of seven advantages. However, he wrote:
1) It is the perfect formula for the child.
2) It provides immunity against several diseases.
3) It is always the right temperature.
4) It is inexpensive.
5) It bonds the child to mother, and vice versa.
6) It is always available as needed. And then the student was stuck. Finally, in desperation, just before the bell rang indicating the end of the test, he wrote:
7) It comes in two attractive containers and it's high enough off the ground where the cat can't get it. He was awarded an A.

Top 10 things that sound dirty in golf but aren't
1 - Nuts...my shaft is bent.
2 - After 18 holes I can barely walk.
3 - You really whacked the hell out of that sucker.
4 - Look at the size of his putter.
5 - Keep your head down and spread your legs a bit more.
6 - Mind if I join your threesome?
7 - Stand with your back turned and drop it.
8 - My hands are so sweaty I can't get a good grip.
9- Nice stroke, but your follow through has a lot to be desired.
10 - Hold up...I need to wash my balls first.

Hilary Clinton fell and hit her skull on the floor. Reporter asks Bill Clinton, "How's Hillary's head"?
Bill: "Well, she's no Monica..."

Pakistani Suicide Hotline - "Thank you for calling the suicide hotline. Can you drive a truck"?

I went to see a Muslim tribute band last night They were

called "Bomb Jovi". They were brilliant Their last song "Living on a Prayer Mat" almost brought the house down Then this Muslim bloke started bragging about how he had the entire Koran on DVD I was interested, so I asked, "Can you burn me a copy Well, that was when the trouble started.........

A dog walks into the telegraph office and says " Hi I would like to send the following message. 'Woof Woof Woof Woof Woof Woof Woof Woof ' ."
The clerk says " Did you know you could send another woof for the same price?'
The dog replies "Don't be silly, that wouldn't make any sense."

I asked my personal trainer "Can you teach me to do the splits?"
He said, "How flexible are you?"
I said " I can't make it on Tuesdays."
T-Shirt sayings....
Beer is good, but beers are better.
Alcohol doesn't solve problems but then again, neither does milk.
With enough thrust, pigs fly just fine.
If a man says he will fixit, there is no need to remind him every six months.
My train of thought has left the station.
Be yourself - everyone else is taken.
The last thing I wan to do is hurt you - but it is still on my list.
If life gives you melons you might be dyslexic.
I can explain it to you but I can't understand it for you.
Pass me a beer and watch me get awesome.
Two wrongs don't make a right but three lefts make a right.
Silently correcting your grammar.
Statistics mean never having to say you're certain.
6 out of 7 dwarves are not Happy.
Don't worry about Zombies - they are looking for brains.
Never trust an atom - they make up everything.
Back in my day we had nine planets.

Take me to your litre.

Guitarists fret over everything.

Earth without art is just "eh".

Well another day passed and I didn't use Calculus once.

I'm not lazy - I'm physically conservative.

What I really need are minions.

Two crows = attempted murder.

Either you like bacon, or you are wrong.

Libraries - shhhhh happens.

I'm so busy I don't know if I found a rope or lost a horse.

Never use a preposition to end a sentence with.

Let's eat Grandma. Let's eat, Grandma. Punctuation saves lives.

Without music the world would B flat.

It was me. I let the dogs out.

In dog beers I have only had one.

I'm perfect. You adjust.

Listen and Silent have the same letters - coincidence?

iTired - there's a nap for that.

I've learned so much from my mistakes - I think I'll make a few more.

If you can't stand the heat, don't tickle the dragon.

To save time, let's assume I know everything.

Resistance is not futile. It's voltage divided by current.

Irony. The opposite of wrinkly.

Santa's helpers are subordinate Clauses.

A backward poet writes inverse.

I regret not developing my photographic memory.

Her bootlegging was illegal, but I loved her still.

My theory on inertia has no momentum.

I before E except when eight feisty neighbours seize a surfeit of weighty heifers.

The past, the present and the future walk into a bar. It was tense.

A man shows up to the doctor with two carrots in his nose, and celery sticking out of his nose.

"Something is not right." he says
The doctor replies " I think you might have an eating problem."

A man walks into a zoo.
The only animal in the entire zoo is a dog.
It's a shitzhu.

Students in an advanced Biology class were taking their mid-term exam. The last question was, 'Name seven advantages of Mother's Milk.' The question was worth 70 points or none at all. One student, in particular, was hard put to think of seven advantages. However, he wrote:

1) It is the perfect formula for the child.

2) It provides immunity against several diseases.

3) It is always the right temperature.

4) It is inexpensive.

5) It bonds the child to mother, and vice versa.

6) It is always available as needed.

And then the student was stuck. Finally, in desperation, just before the bell rang indicating the end of the test, he wrote:

7) It comes in two attractive containers and it's high enough off the ground where the cat can't get it. He was awarded an A.

I don't claim to know much about Lifesaving, but if anyone's going to bring this guy back to life, my money would be on the Girl on the Right!

The waiter at the Post goes up to 4 Jewish ladies eating dinner and asks, "Is anything alright?"

The guy walks in to the doctors office with carrots sticking out of his nose and celery out of his ears "I just don't feel good, Doc." he says. The physician pauses and says "Maybe you aren't eating right."

A lunatic walks in to the bar dressed as a pirate with a steering wheel down the front of his pants. "Arrr bar tender I will have a rum!" he yells. The bar tender serves him then says, "Why the steering wheel in the front of your pants?" The pirate looks at him with a crazy leer then down at it and says "Arrr it's driving me nuts!"

A pilot walks into a bar and takes a seat next to a very attractive woman. He gives her a quick glance then casually looks at his watch for a moment. The woman notices this and asks, "Is your date running late?" "No," he replies, "I just got this state-of-the-art watch, and I was just testing it."
 The intrigued woman says, "A state-of-the-art watch? What's so special about it?" The pilot says, "It uses alpha waves to talk to me telepathically." The lady says, "What's it telling you now?"
 Well, it says you're not wearing any panties."
 The woman giggles and replies, "Well it must be broken because I am wearing panties!" The pilot smirks, taps his watch and says, "Darn thing's an hour fast."

1. I'm reading a great book on anti-gravity. I can't put it down.

2. I have a new theory on inertia but it doesn't seem to be gaining momentum.

3. Schrodinger's cat walks into a bar. And doesn't.

4. Why can't atheists solve exponential equations? Because they don't believe in higher powers.

5. Do you know the name Pavlov? It rings a bell.

6. A group of protesters in front of a physics lab -"What do we want?" "Time travel" "When do we want it?" "Irrelevant."

7. What does a subatomic duck say? Quark!

8. A neutron walks into a bar and asks how much for a beer. Bartender replies "For you, no charge".

9. Two atoms are walking along. One of them says: "Oh, no, I think I lost an electron." "Are you sure?" "Yes, I'm positive."

10. An optimist sees a glass half full. A pessimist sees it half empty. An engineer sees it twice as large as it needs to be.

A man walks into a zoo.
The only animal in the entire zoo is a dog.
It's a shitzhu.

A biologist, a chemist, and a statistician are out hunting. The biologist shoots at a deer and misses 5 ft to the left, the chemist takes a shot and misses 5 ft to the right, and the statistician yells, 'We got 'im!' "
Why it's funny: Because it's mean.

Husband and wife had a tiff. Wife called up her mom and said, "He fought with me again, I am coming to live with you." Mom said, "No darling, he must pay for his mistake. I am coming to live with you.

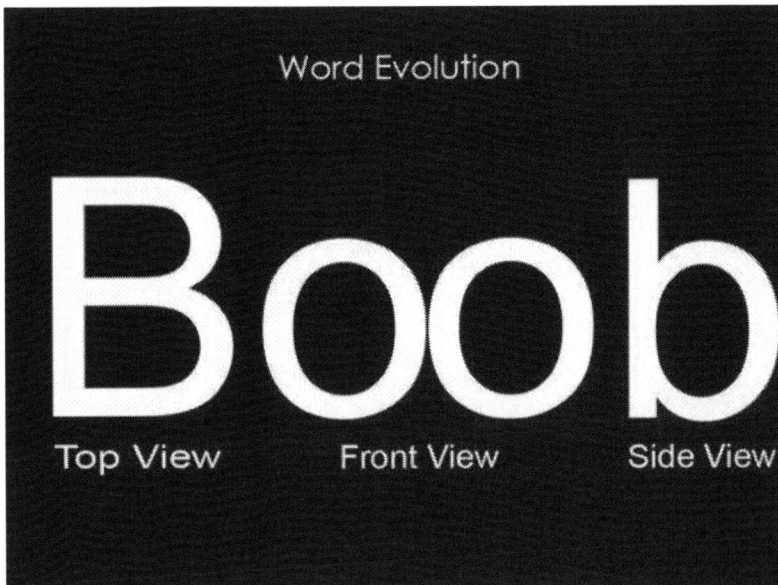

Word Evolution

Boob

Top View   Front View   Side View

To write with a broken pencil is pointless.

When fish are in schools they sometimes take debate.

A thief who stole a calendar got twelve months.

When the smog lifts in Los Angeles, UCLA.

The professor discovered that her theory of earthquakes was on shaky ground.

The batteries were given out free of charge.

A dentist and a manicurist married. They fought tooth and nail.

A will is a dead giveaway.

If you don't pay your exorcist you can get repossessed.

With her marriage, she got a new name and a dress.

Show me a piano falling down a mineshaft and I'll show you A-flat miner.

You are stuck with your debt if you can't budge it.

Local Area Network in Australia: The LAN down under.

A boiled egg is hard to beat.

When you've seen one shopping centre you've seen a mall.

Police were called to a day care where a three-year-old was resisting a rest.

Did you hear about the fellow whose whole left side was cut off? He's all right now.

If you take a laptop computer for a run you could jog your memory.

A bicycle can't stand alone; it is two-tired.

In a democracy it's your vote that counts; in feudalism, it's your Count that votes.

When a clock is hungry it goes back four seconds.

The guy who fell onto an upholstery machine was fully recovered.

He had a photographic memory which was never developed.

Those who get too big for their britches will be exposed in the end.

When she saw her first strands of grey hair, she thought she'd dye.

Acupuncture: a jab well done.

T-Shirt sayings....
Beer is good, but beers are better.
Alcohol doesn't solve problems but then again, neither does milk.
With enough thrust, pigs fly just fine.
If a man says he will fixit, there is no need to remind him every six months.
My train of thought has left the station.
Be yourself - everyone else is taken.
The last thing I wan to do is hurt you - but it is still on my list.
If life gives you melons you might be dyslexic.
I can explain it to you but I can't understand it for you.
Pass me a beer and watch me get awesome.
Two wrongs don't make a right but three lefts make a right.
Silently correcting your grammar.
Statistics mean never having to say you're certain.
6 out of 7 dwarves are not Happy.
Don't worry about Zombies - they are looking for brains.
Never trust an atom - they make up everything.
Back in my day we had nine planets.
Take me to your litre.
Guitarists fret over everything.
Earth without art is just "eh".
Well another day passed and I didn't use Calculus once.
I'm not lazy - I'm physically conservative.
What I really need are minions.
Two crows = attempted murder.
Either you like bacon, or you are wrong.
Libraries - shhhhh happens.
I'm so busy I don't know if I found a rope or lost a horse.
Never use a preposition to end a sentence with.
Let's eat Grandma. Let's eat, Grandma. Punctuation saves lives.

Without music the world would B flat.

It was me. I let the dogs out.

In dog beers I have only had one.

I'm perfect. You adjust.

Listen and Silent have the same letters - coincidence?

iTired - there's a nap for that.

I've learned so much from my mistakes - I think I'll make a few more.

If you can't stand the heat, don't tickle the dragon.

To save time, let's assume I know everything.

Resistance is not futile. It's voltage divided by current.

Irony. The opposite of wrinkly.

Santa's helpers are subordinate Clauses.

A backward poet writes inverse.

I regret not developing my photographic memory.

Her bootlegging was illegal, but I loved her still.

My theory on inertia has no momentum.

I before E except when eight feisty neighbours seize a surfeit of weighty heifers.

The past, the present and the future walk into a bar. It was tense.

'I' before 'E' except when there's a feisty heist on weird beige foreign neighbours reinventing protein at their leisure.

What do you call a snake that keeps falling over?
"A Reptile Dysfunction "

A female Mountie pulled over a drunken Newfie fisherman driving home down a back road. She said, "You're under arrest. Anything you say, can and will be held against you."
"Tits!" replied the Newfie.

Why does Waldo wear stripes? Because he doesn't want to be spotted.

Why doesn't a bear wear shoes? Because he goes bear foot.

What do you when you find a space man? You park in it man.

Why didn't the lifeguard save the hippie? He was too far out.

Dyslexic man walks into a bra.

Technically we are all half centaurs.

Why do the French have so many wars? So they can win one every now and then.

Why does Waldo wear stripes?
So he won't be spotted.

How many surrealists does it take to screw in a light bulb?
Two. One to hold the giraffe and the other to fill the bathtub with brightly coloured machine tools.

MUTE   OFF

┌──────────── GIVE ME ────────────┐

BEER   SEX   FOOD

MASSAGE   STOP   SLEEP
           WINGING

◁   SAY NO   REMOVE   SAY YES   ▷
              CLOTHES

SHOP   CLEAN   LEAVE

PMS OFF   STOP NAGGING

                +
             BOOBS
                −

JVC

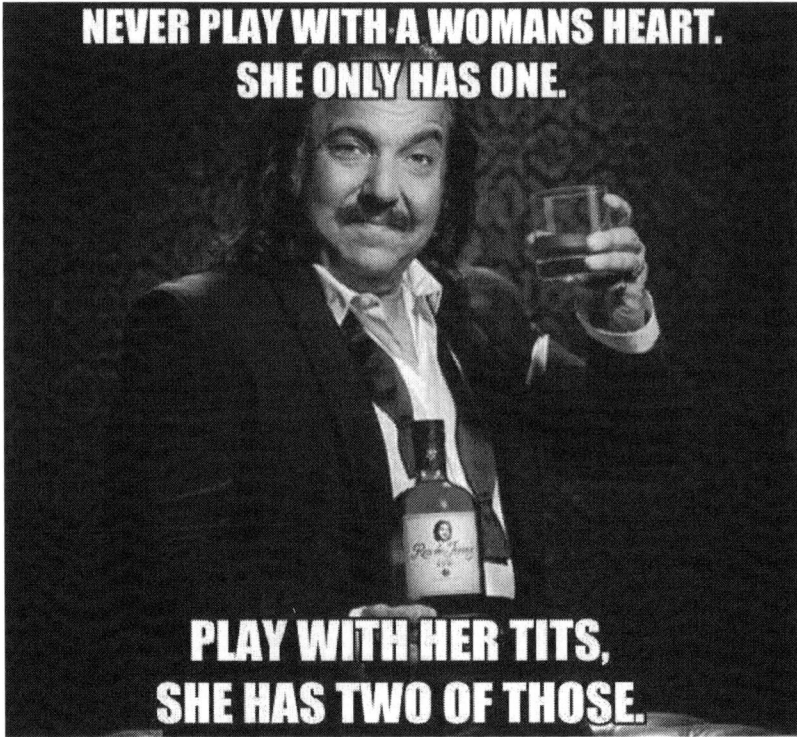

NEVER PLAY WITH A WOMANS HEART.
SHE ONLY HAS ONE.

PLAY WITH HER TITS,
SHE HAS TWO OF THOSE.

A mechanic was removing a cylinder head from the engine of a Honda. When he spotted a well known cardiologist in the workshop. The Cardiologist was there waiting for the service manager to come and take a look at his car when the mechanic shouted across the garage, "Hey Doc, want to take a look at this?" The cardiologist, a bit surprised walked over to where the mechanic was working on the Honda. The mechanic straightened up, wiped his hands on a rag and said, "So Doc, look at this motor. I opened its heart, took the valves out, Repaired or replaced anything damaged and then put everything back in and when I finished, it worked just like new. So how is it that I make $54,000 a year and you make $1.7M, when you and I are doing basically the same work?" The cardiologist paused, leaned over and whispered to the mechanic: "Try doing it with the engine running, Son." "

Optimism is the best
Way to see life

One typo can destroy your life. A husband wrote a message to his wife on his official trip and forgot to add 'e' at the end of a word.

"I am having such a wonderful time! Wish you were her!"

What do you call a masturbating cow?

Beef stroking off.

What is the name of the Chinese billionaire?
Cha Ching.

What did the hungry clock do?
It went back four seconds.

Birthday Wishes....

I'm not making any age related jokes because I genuinely feel bad about how old you are.

May your birthday be devoid of cute animals and soul shredding word play.

May you live long enough to shit yourself.

Today's the anniversary of you being expelled from your mother's uterus.

You've reached an age that has no significance at all.

Happy birthday to one of the few people whose birthday I can remember without a Facebook reminder.

I remember when you weren't so disturbingly old.

Let's over celebrate your birthday.

Even though we are no longer sleeping together, Happy Birthday.

Wishing you a happy birthday makes me feel gay.

This is the perfect day to thank me for remembering your birthday.

Other Cards...

Sorry in advance for doing a ton of stupid shit.

Sorry you don't understand how important I am.

Congratulations on defying marriage statistics.

It's remarkable how long we have tolerated each other.

If I still had a soul, you'd be its mate.

Happy Anniversary to a couple that almost never makes me physically ill.

Congratulations on your new job that you probably won't like any better.

Dad, you've always been like a father to me.

Sorry you're feeling like such a pussy.

Get well soon because your cough is fucking disgusting.

Good luck finding shameful entry-level employment.

Congratulations on sleeping with the same person for eternity.

Congratulations on probably not dying alone.

It's going to be a great first marriage.

I hope a mediocre Mother's Day brunch can help negate 364 days of smug ingratitude.

You're going to be a great MILF.

I think of you every time I browse my cell phone on the toilet.

I will be your friend no matter what you put in your anus.

What is the name of the summer activity for Jewish kids who have ADHD?
Concentration Camp.

Guy stops at gas station to put air in his tires. He complains to attendant that it used to be free but now costs fifty cents. Attendant: "I guess that's inflation for you..."

APTITUDE TEST

1. If you went to bed at 8 o'clock at night and set the alarm to get you up at 9 o'clock, how many hours of sleep would this permit you?

2. Do they have a fourth of July in England?

3. How many birthdays does the average person have?

4. Why can't a man living in Winston-Salem, North Carolina be buried west of the Mississippi?

5. If you have one match, and entered a room in which there was a kerosene lamp, an oil heater, and a wood-burning stove, which would you light first?

6. Some months have 30 days-some have 31 - How many have 28 days?

7. If a doctor gave you three pills and told you. to take one every 1/2 hour, how long would they last?

8. A man builds a house with four sides to it, and it is rectangular in shape - Each side has a southern exposure - A big bear came wandering by - What color is the bear?

9. How far can a dog run into the woods?

10. What four words appear on all denominations of U.S. coins?

11. What is the maximum number of players that can be on the field during any inning of a world series baseball game? How many outs in an inning?

12. I have in my hand two U.S. coins which total 55 cents in

value. Bear in mind that one of them is not a nickel. What are the two coins?

13. A farmer had 17 sheep, all but 9 died - How many were left?

14. Two men played checkers - Each played five games and each won the same number of games, and there were no draws - How can this be?

15. Take two apples from three apples, what do you have?

16. An archaeologist claimed he found some coins of gold dated 46 B.C.--Did he?

17. A woman gives a beggar 50 cents. The woman is the beggar's sister, but the beggar is not the woman's brother. How come?

18. How many animals of each species did Moses take aboard the ark with him?

19. Divide 30 by 1/2 and add ten. What do you have?

20. Is it legal in California for a man to marry his widow's sister?

Scientist: I tried to publish my paper about cloning, but the referee said they couldn't reproduce the results.

Latin abbreviations > 2015 English:
e.g. = like,
i.e. = you know,
etc. = or whatever,
et al. = or whoever,
cf. = check out,
viz. = you know

NEGOTIATION LESSON

Jim wanted desperately to have sex with this really cute, really hot girl in his office, but she was dating someone else.
One day Jim got so frustrated that he went to her and said, 'I'll give you $100 if you let me have sex with you.'
The girl looked at him and then said, 'NO.'
Jim said, 'I'll be real fast. I'll throw the money on the floor, you bend down, and I'll finish by the time you've picked it up.'
She thought for a moment and said that she would consult with her boyfriend. She called him and explained the situation.
Her boyfriend says, 'Ask him for $200, and pick up the money really fast. He won't even be able to get his pants down.'
She agreed and accepts the proposal.
Over half an hour goes by and the boyfriend is waiting for his girlfriend's call. Finally, after 45 minutes the boyfriend calls and asks,
'What happened?'
Still breathing hard, she managed to reply, 'The bastard had all quarters!'
Negotiation lesson: Always consider a business proposition in its entirety before agreeing to it and getting screwed.

A young blonde girl in her late teens, wanting to earn some extra money for the summer, decided to hire herself out as a "handy woman" and started canvassing a nearby well-to-do neighbourhood. She went to the front door of the first house and asked the owner if he had any odd jobs for her to do. "Well, I guess I could use somebody to paint the porch. How much will you charge me?" Delighted, the girl quickly responded, "How about $50?" The man agreed and told her that the paint and brushes and everything she would need were in the garage. The man's wife, hearing the conversation, said to her husband, "Does she realize that our porch goes ALL the way around the house?" "That's a bit cynical, isn't it?" he responded. The wife replied, "You're right. I guess I'm starting to believe all those dumb blonde jokes." A few hours later the blonde came to the door to collect her money. "You're finished already??" the startled husband asked. "Yes," the blonde replied, "and I even had paint left over so I gave it two coats." Impressed, the man reached into his pocket for the $50 and handed it to her along with a $10 tip. "Thank you," the blonde said, "And, by the way, it's not a Porch, it's a Lexus."

Late Monday morning, the battered fighter pilot finally regained consciousness... He found himself in agonizing pain in the base hospital's ICU, with tubes up every fundamental orifice, wires monitoring every function and a gorgeous nurse hovering over him. He remembered he'd been in a serious flying accident on Saturday. The nurse gave the fighter pilot a serious, deep look straight into the eyes, and he heard her slowly say, "You may not feel anything from the waist down." Somehow he managed to mumble in reply, "Can I feel your tits, then?"

Is it crazy how saying sentences backwards creates backwards sentences saying how crazy it is?

Q: How many flies does it take to screw in a light bulb?
A: Two, but how did they get in there?

Technically, we are all half Centaurs.

Q. Why have the French had so many civil wars?

A. So they can win one every now and then.

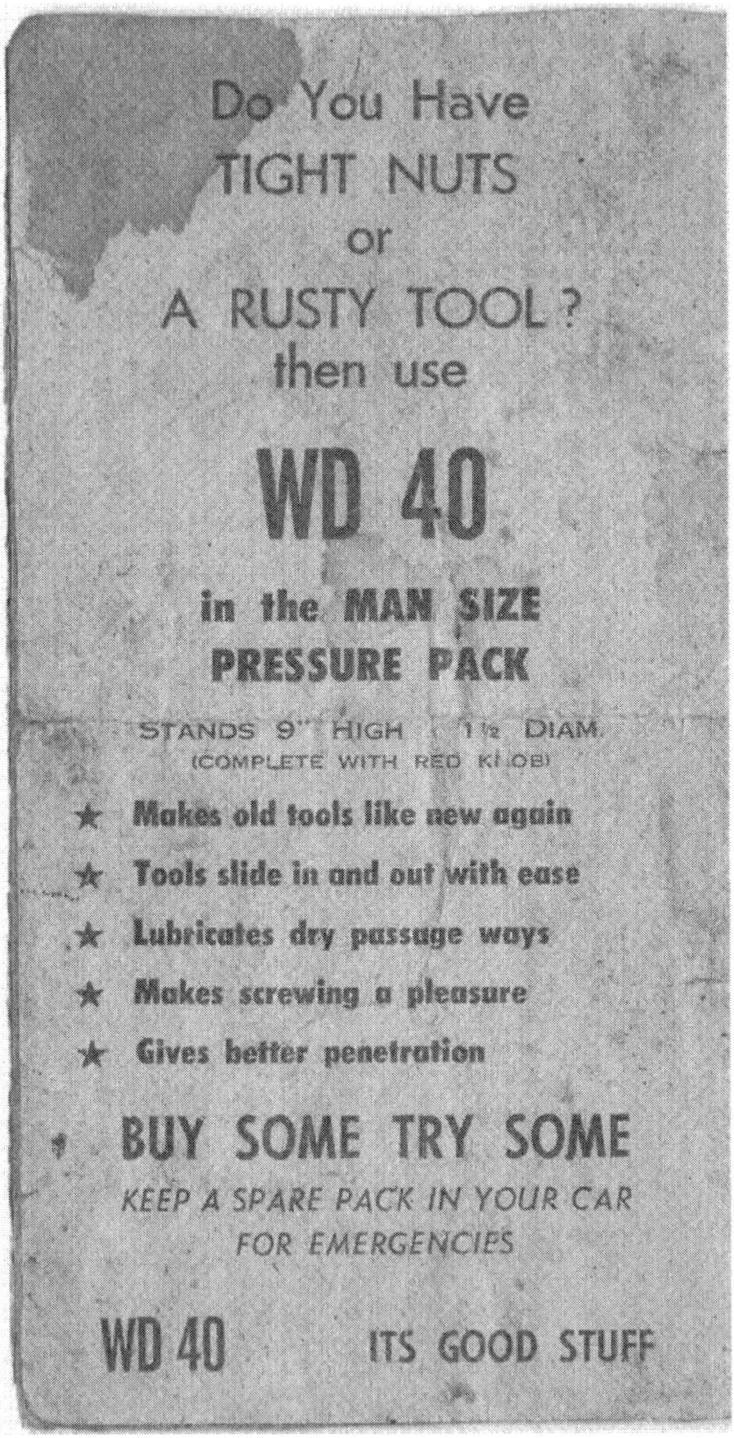

Do You Have
TIGHT NUTS
or
A RUSTY TOOL?
then use

WD 40

in the MAN SIZE PRESSURE PACK

STANDS 9" HIGH 1½ DIAM.
(COMPLETE WITH RED KNOB)

★ Makes old tools like new again

★ Tools slide in and out with ease

★ Lubricates dry passage ways

★ Makes screwing a pleasure

★ Gives better penetration

BUY SOME TRY SOME

KEEP A SPARE PACK IN YOUR CAR
FOR EMERGENCIES

WD 40   ITS GOOD STUFF

One bright, sunny Sunday, a husband & wife decided that they were long overdue for "matters of the heart" ("les affaires de cœur"). The only way to pull off a Sunday afternoon "quickie" with their 8-year-old son in their apartment was to send him out on the balcony with a Popsicle. They did so and told him to report to them on all the neighborhood activities.
 "There's a car being towed from the parking lot," he shouted. He began his commentary as his parents put their plan into operation. "An ambulance just drove by!" "Looks like the Andersons have company," he called out.
"Matt's riding a new bike! Looks like the Sanders are moving! Jason is on his skate board!" After a few moments he announced, "The Coopers are having sex again." Startled, his mother and dad immediately shot up in their bed. The father cautiously called outside, "How do you know they're having sex?"
"Jimmy Cooper is standing out on his balcony with a Popsicle."

The difference ...between male and female priorities....

After a tiring day, a commuter settled down in his seat and closed his eyes. As the train rolled out of the station, the young woman sitting next to him pulled out her cell phone and started talking in a loud voice: "Hi sweetheart. It's Sue. I'm on the train". "Yes, I know it's the six thirty and not the four thirty, but I had a long meeting". "No, honey, not with that Kevin from the accounting office. It was with the boss". "No sweetheart, you're the only one in my life". "Yes, I'm sure, cross my heart!" Fifteen minutes later, she was still talking loudly. When the man sitting next to her had enough, he leaned over and said into the phone, "Sue, hang up the phone and come back to bed." Sue doesn't use her cell phone in public any longer.

A chicken farmer went to the local bar.
He sat next to a woman and ordered champagne.
The woman said: "How strange, I also just ordered a glass of champagne.
" What a coincidence " - said the farmer, who added: "It is a special day for me.
I am celebrating..."It is a special day for me too.
I am also celebrating!" - said the woman.
What a coincidence" - said the farmer.
While they toasted, the man asked: "What are you celebrating?"
My husband and I have been trying to have a child for years, and today, my gynecologist told me that I was pregnant!"
What a coincidence!" - said the man - "I am a chicken farmer and for years, all my hens were infertile, but now they are all set to lay fertilized eggs.
This is awesome!" - said the woman. "What did you do for your chickens to become fertile?"
"I used a different rooster" - he said. The woman smiled and said: "What a coincidence..."

Did you hear about the two antennas that got married?
The wedding wasn't much, but the reception was great!

A man got on a bus with both of his front trouser pockets full of golf balls .
He sat down next to a beautiful (you guessed it) blonde.
The puzzled blonde kept looking at him and his bulging pockets.
Finally, after many glances from her, he said, "It's golf balls."
The blonde continued to look at him, thinking deeply about what he had said.
After several minutes, not being able to contain her curiosity any longer,
she asked, "Does it hurt as much as tennis elbow?

Why didn't the lifeguard save the hippie?
He was too far out...

A female Mountie pulled over a drunk Newfie fisherman driving home down a back road.
She said, "You're under arrest. Anything you say, can and will be held against you."
"Tits!" replied the Newfie.

 A man was telling his buddy, "You won't believe what happened last night... My daughter walked into the living room and said, 'Dad, cancel my allowance immediately, forget my college tuition loan, rent my room out, throw all my clothes out the window; take my TV, and my laptop.   Please take any of my jewelry to the Salvation Army or Cash Converters. Then, sell my car, take my front door key away from me and throw me out of the house. Then, disown me and never talk to me again.   And don't forget to write me out of your will and leave my share to any charity you choose.' "
"Holy Smokes," replied the friend, "she actually said that?"
"Well, she didn't put it quite like that, she actually said...
'Dad, meet my new boyfriend - Mohammed. We're going to work together on Trudeau's election campaign!' "

I found this humerus

Manufactured by Amazon.ca
Bolton, ON